Regulating Risk

The Science and Politics of Risk

Regulating Risk

The Science and Politics of Risk

A Conference Summary

Edited by Thomas A. Burke, Nga L. Tran,
Jane S. Roemer, and Carol J. Henry

National Safety Council

ILSI
International Life Sciences INSTITUTE

© 1993 by the International Life Sciences Institute. All rights reserved.
Published 1993. Printed in the United States of America.

International Life Sciences Institute/ILSI Risk Science Institute,
1126 Sixteenth St., NW, Washington, DC 20036

National Safety Council, 1121 Spring Lake Drive, Itasca, IL 60143

Library of Congress Cataloging in Publication Data
93-061119

ISBN 0-944398-13-8

CONTENTS

Part 5

Part 6

Part 7

Part 8

Introductory Comments

I n June 1991, the National Safety Council in partnership with the ILSI Risk Science Institute held a two-day conference, called "Regulating Risk," in Washington, D.C. The meeting was subtitled "The Science and Politics of Risk" to reflect the complexity—and indeed the controversy—of the subject.

In deciding to hold a conference on the subject of health, safety, and environmental risk, the conference sponsors sought to bring together experts and interested parties from a broad range of disciplines to discuss issues common to all decision making on risk. The goal was to advance the dialogue about risk and to contribute to the larger aim of improving how we manage it.

This report is a summary of the presentations made at the conference. The subjects covered and questions raised at the June 1991 meeting continue to reflect the many factors involved in societal decisions about risk: What are the roles—and limitations—of science in understanding risk? How do federal agencies charged with safeguarding the public from risk decide which hazards to address? Are traditional approaches to assessing risk working to promote and enhance public safety? What is the influence of politics, economics, and perceptions on risk policy? How does the public perceive risk, and what role do the media play in creating those perceptions?

When discussions were first undertaken for the conference, a publication resulting from the meeting was not part of the plan. In the course of the meeting, however, the conference organizers more fully realized that the material being presented was unique in scope and might well benefit a much larger audience than the 300-plus scientists, managers, regulators, communicators, and others who attended the conference. The core of a valuable publication was there: a comprehensive treatment on critical issues in risk by many of the most respected authorities in risk assessment, management, communication, and regulation.

A panel of editors was named, and we went to work to create a publication that would capture the essence and breadth of the conference. We knew that it was unrealistic to ask all of the speakers to reconstruct formal papers from their presentation notes or drafts. Indeed, we believed that a publication that captured the essential points of each presentation and that reflected the breadth of thought and opinion at the meeting would be of far greater value than a traditional conference proceedings monograph.

Fortunately, all of the presentations were recorded and transcribed. Nga Tran, a graduate student in the Johns Hopkins School of Hygiene and Public Health, helped us comb through the transcription, identify the important points made by each speaker, and summarize their presentations. These drafts were submitted to the speakers, who were given an opportunity to make further changes and asked to return their approved drafts for copy editing and production.

Nga's enormous contribution to this effort cannot be underestimated or overstated; indeed, the editorial panel agreed that she richly deserved a position on the editorial roster. Roberta Gutman, ILSI Press's managing editor, and Walter Ludwig, the press's director, also contributed importantly to the editing and production of this book.

We also want to take this opportunity to thank the two sponsors of the conference: the National Safety Council and ILSI Risk Science Institute. The Illinois-based council, founded in 1913, is a nonprofit, nongovernmental public service organization that serves as the nation's most extensive source of safety information. Originally concerned with preventing accidental deaths and injuries in the workplace, the council has expanded its efforts to encompass highway and off-the-job safety, including occupational and environmental health along with general wellness.

The ILSI Risk Science Institute is a public, nonprofit research foundation within the International Life Sciences Institute. Established in 1985, the Risk Science Institute seeks to improve risk assessment by strengthening the scientific principles on which assessments are based. The institute works toward this goal by facilitating cooperation among scientists in government, academia, and industry through a wide range of research activities, workshops and conferences, publications, and educational programs worldwide.

This conference on risk was undertaken at the suggestion and with the support of the National Safety Council's Industrial Division volunteer leadership. In particular, we would like to recognize division member Fred A. Manuele for the assistance and steady encouragement he provided.

We also wish to acknowledge the role of the advisory committee in the success of the conference. Committee members included Frederick W. Allen, Theodore Glickman, Bernard D. Goldstein, John D. Graham, Peter Infante, Robert J. Scheuplein, Michael R. Taylor, and Bud Ward. Their affiliations are given at the back of this book in a full listing of the committee.

Finally, we would like to thank National Safety Council staff members Sharon Vojtek, Stacy Johnson, and Sophie LoBue, and ILSI staff member Diane Dalisera. Their assistance in arranging and presenting the conference was invaluable.

THOMAS A. BURKE
Johns Hopkins School of Hygiene and Public Health

JANE S. ROEMER
National Safety Council

CAROL J. HENRY
ILSI Risk Science Institute

PART 1

Managing Risk in a Risky World

INTRODUCTION BY JANE S. ROEMER

I n general, we all know the meaning of the word "risk": it is the measure of probability of a harm or loss. As individuals, we weigh risks concerning our health and safety every day of our lives and make personal decisions based on the outcome.

For each of us, the risk equation is a little different. Imagine, then, the potential for complications when we are talking about societal, rather than personal, risk, and we begin to see why the subject of risk is so challenging. With societal risk, it is not simply one individual weighing his or her own interests against a possible harm; it is society balancing competing concerns, determining which risks are acceptable and deciding how safe is safe.

As our scientific knowledge has grown, so have demands on government to control risks to our health, safety, and environment. In just the last two decades, entirely new federal and state agencies have been created to address newly recognized areas of concern.

Moreover, as the public has become better informed and more engaged in the debate, our definition of "acceptable" risk has changed. Some risks once considered a matter of personal choice now are seen as having societal consequences, economic and otherwise—hence the advent of mandatory safety belt use laws and restrictions on smoking in public.

It is no surprise, then, that government's involvement in risk decisions cuts across many subject areas, from traffic safety to environmental health, from workplace safety to the foods we eat. In all of these fields, the risk equation starts with information based in science but quickly moves to the arena of "policy making." Along the way, factors of economics, public perceptions, law, ethics, and politics are brought into the mix.

As this conference report shows, there are many different views on how to better address and manage risk. The conference did not attempt to provide single answers to the questions that were raised. Rather, the objective was to present a range of opinions from many perspectives by some of the leading risk scientists and policy thinkers of the day.

The four papers in this introductory section are summaries of keynote and other special addresses at the meeting. The speakers—risk educator Peter M. Sandman, President Bush's science advisor, D. Allan Bromley, consumer advocate Ralph Nader, and F. Henry Habicht II, who was then deputy administrator of the U.S. Environmental Protection Agency—offer four distinct and provocative interpretations on the role, and limitations, of risk assessment and management. In the report's concluding chapter, conference advisor Dr. Thomas A. Burke of the Johns Hopkins School of Hygiene and Public Health reviews the presentations and provides his thoughts on conference themes and on directions for the future.

It is hoped that the summarized presentations in this conference report, and the report's concluding chapter, will stimulate further discussion and action toward developing a new consensus for addressing the complicated and challenging risk decisions that lie ahead.

Jane S. Roemer is executive director of public policy for the National Safety Council.

Definitions of Risk:
Managing the Outrage, Not Just the Hazard

• PETER M. SANDMAN

THE FIELD OF RISK MANAGEMENT has evolved as a linear three-step process in the following order: risk assessment, risk management, and risk communication. This order of business, however, is not working because the public is not content to be at the end of the process flow.

There are risks that frighten people, even though the risk assessors tell us people shouldn't be frightened. We must be cautious in criticizing the public for this, for several reasons. First, the risk assessors have sometimes been wrong. There are many historical examples where the consensus of the experts was wrong and the public and a minority of experts turned out to be right. Second, there are some environmental risks that are gradual, delayed, geometric, or made much worse by simultaneous exposure to other risks, so that by the time we have good data it might be too late. Third, quantitative risk assessment is often wielded with a bias; the public is right to be skeptical when the people who assert that a risk is small have a stake in its being small.

Nonetheless, most of us here agree that the mismatch between the public's concern and real damage to health or the ecosystem is a genuine one. The Environmental Protection Agency has been spending money where the public thinks it should, not where the experts think the problems are most serious. In most though not all cases, the experts are going to turn out to be closer to correct than the public.

People in industry, government, and academia who are pushing for a better resolution of that mismatch are pushing for something worth achieving. They are pushing, however, in the wrong direction. They argue that the task is to educate the public—to teach people that they are wrong and the experts are right. This is a step forward from the conventional preference of most experts to ignore the public altogether. But this one-way approach to education makes the crucial mistake of assuming that the public is simply wrong about risk. In fact, the public is focusing on aspects of risk that the experts have defined out of the problem.

What the risk assessors mean by risk is not what anybody else means by risk. To a risk assessor, risk is a multiplication of magnitude—how bad is it when it happens?—and probability—how likely is it to happen? Let's call that "hazard," and let's call what the public means by risk "outrage." In outrage terms, a big outrage is a big risk. The experts focus on hazard and ignore outrage, whereas the public focuses on outrage and ignores hazard.

This suggests a new definition of risk: hazard plus outrage. There are somewhere between 20 and 40 components of outrage that affect the public's view of risk and that should be considered part of what we mean by risk. Twelve of these are listed in Table 1. We have two decades of data indicating that these factors are important components of our society's definition of risk.

RISK = HAZARD + OUTRAGE

Table 1. Twelve principal outrage components

"SAFE"	"RISKY"
Voluntary	Coerced
Natural	Industrial
Familiar	Exotic
Not memorable	Memorable
Not dreaded	Dreaded
Chronic	Catastrophic
Knowable	Unknowable
Individually controlled	Controlled by others
Fair	Unfair
Morally irrelevant	Morally relevant
Trustworthy sources	Untrustworthy sources
Responsive process	Unresponsive process

The public wants high-outrage risks taken more seriously than low-outrage risks.

The problem is that policy makers are not willing to accept, and have not yet figured out how to cope with, a public that cares more about outrage than hazard. Our continuing to ignore the public's outrage concerns is literally irrational. It is just as irrational as the public's continuing to ignore our technical concerns. Note that this is not a battle between data and emotions, but between one kind of data and another. In most risk controversies, in fact, we have better data on outrage than on hazard.

It is true that the public often misunderstands the hazard, but this is the effect of outrage, not its cause. People misunderstand the data because they are outraged. If we correct the misunderstanding without reducing the outrage, we have not changed their policy preferences. The public wants high-outrage risks taken more seriously than low-outrage risks. Thus, managing outrage is as important as managing hazard, and managing risk is managing both hazard and outrage.

The paradox of hazard versus outrage is very important. Environmentalists and media generate outrage, nurture outrage on purpose. Industry and government nurture it by accident, by ignoring it. When we ignore outrage, we exacerbate it. When we pay attention to it, we reduce it. Managing outrage works.

How can we achieve technically optimal policies? By merging technical with political and psychological concerns at the beginning. Quantitative risk assessment is a good thing; it is not perfect, but it is better than nothing. It is the best tool we have for deciding how big a hazard is. But if we use it as an excuse for paying less attention to the public, less attention to outrage, then the outrage is going to increase. The gap between the public's and experts' concerns will increase, and quantitative risk assessment will be discredited in the process. An autocratic, unresponsive, untrustworthy risk manager is still a tyrant, even if he or she has better data.

We should distinguish two kinds of risk assessment: "hazard assessment" and "outrage assessment." We should try to develop a risk management process that legitimizes both and considers both. The outcome can be a simultaneous increase in our ability to protect public health and the environment and our ability to maintain a democratic society where people respond rationally, calmly, perhaps even trustingly, to risk.

Peter M. Sandman, Ph.D., founded and directed the Environmental Communication Research Program (now called the Center for Environmental Communication) at Rutgers University until 1992. For a fuller explanation of the hazard-versus-outrage distinction, write Dr. Sandman at 54 Gray Cliff Road, Newton Centre, MA 02159 (617-630-0385), or write for a Center for Environmental Communication Publications List at P.O. Box 231, Cook College, Rutgers University, New Brunswick, NJ 08903 (908-932-8795). This summary of Dr. Sandman's keynote address was written by Ms. Nga Tran, then edited and approved by Dr. Sandman.

Risk Assessment:
The Need for a Common Perspective

• D. ALLAN BROMLEY

OST PEOPLE TEND TO SEE THINGS as 100 percent safe, as 100 percent dangerous and to be avoided at all costs, or as having a 50/50 chance of being harmful. It is this view that makes risk assessment extraordinarily difficult: an adverse event with a one in a million chance of occurring can be viewed as having a 50/50 chance of occurring.

This disjointed public view of risk is inevitably reflected in many regulations that govern risk assessment and risk management in this country. Furthermore, when laws are being developed, scientific facts are not always the highest priority for attention. As a result, different agencies can regulate the same risk but in different ways and sometimes with quite different standards.

From year to year we learn how to detect all sorts of organic molecules at concentrations that are perhaps two or sometimes three or four orders of magnitude lower than we could have measured in the previous year. We recognize the growing ability of our technologies and the central need to harmonize our risk assessment and risk management approaches. We must be sensitive to the fact that from year to year we will always be able to detect more and more things at lower and lower concentrations. Absent good science and effective communications regarding the meaning of that science, the illogical but inevitable end result of this process is that everything will be judged bad for humans.

One of the approaches that we need to take is to compare risks. We have not done enough risk comparison in the past. The Environmental Protection Agency has been going through a very interesting exercise of beginning to compare risks. Risk comparison is happening in the academic and industrial world and is now beginning to happen in the federal government.

We have to bear in mind that there are no human activities that are 100

People spend a large amount of their time worrying about risks of enormously small magnitude while engaging in all sorts of risky behavior.

percent risk free. If we were to attempt to fully eliminate all the risks to which we are exposed, it would be very difficult for us to progress either technologically or scientifically toward a better life for the American people.

The Federal Coordinating Council for Science, Engineering and Technology is moving to add risk assessment to its other important emphases, which focus on budgets and the development of federal plans in areas such as global change, education, high-performance computing, materials science, and biotechnology. The intent is not to write a manual that the agencies will use in risk assessment but to develop a consensus on the assumptions and principles that should underlie the application of science and technology in support of risk management across the entire spectrum of the federal government. This will mark a substantial change in our approach to risks.

Low public literacy in science and technology is one of the most serious problems this nation faces today, and the issue of public risk perception is tied to it. When we speak of technological risk, we must realize that half of the American public believe in lucky numbers, less than half know that the earth goes around the sun once a year, and American industry spends as much on remedial mathematics education each year as all governments combined spend on direct mathematics education in elementary schools, high schools, and colleges. We have a paradoxical situation in that we still set the style and pace for graduate education worldwide (in fact, graduate education is one of our most important exports). At the college level, however, we are the only developed nation that has no centralized standards for what constitutes a college education. At the precollege level the situation is scandalous. We are giving our children and grandchildren an education of lesser quality than what we received.

The aspect of the breakdown in our educational system that is specifically important to risk assessment and management efforts is the total lack of understanding of either statistics or probability by the average American. People spend a large amount of their time worrying about risks of enormously small magnitude, such as nuclear accidents, while engaging in all sorts of risky behavior, such as smoking, driving, or eating junk food, without giving it a second thought.

Government and the business community must work together to address this educational crisis. The two most important things to do are, first, to get parents reinvolved in the education of their children and, second, to improve the qualifications of teachers in the elementary schools where the problem really resides.

D. Allan Bromley, Ph.D., is Sterling Professor of the Sciences at Yale University. At the time of the conference, he was Assistant to the President of the United States for Science and Technology, on leave from the Henry Ford II Professorship in Physics at Yale.

EPA and Risk: The Next Steps

• F. HENRY HABICHT II

THIS IS AN EXTRAORDINARILY DYNAMIC TIME in environmental policy. The Environmental Protection Agency's approach to environmental protection over its almost 22-year history has been steadily evolving, but perhaps never has there been a time of greater change than the present. The widespread acceptance of pollution prevention and the use of market forces are clear examples of this. Certainly, one of the areas that is changing the most is EPA's approach to risk assessment. We have the opportunity to use environmental risk assessment more constructively—and since risk assessment is fundamental to society-wide approaches to solving environmental problems, it is an opportunity we must take. This means scientifically identifying and reducing the greatest risks to people and the environment without becoming bogged down in fine distinctions or swayed by "crisis of the month" thinking.

A recent Roper poll shows that the environment is still of increasing public concern. Although the EPA's approval rating is improving, there is still an underlying mistrust—particularly of industry, but also of the government—when it comes to how environmental issues are handled. To some, it seems that nothing ever comes off the long list of environmental concerns. Part of this perception surely stems from the fact that in the past there has been a lack of the kind of coherent environmental policy that would enable government to dependably put risks into a context where they can be understood, compared, prioritized, and addressed. We are trying to permanently change this perception.

The joining of environmental policy and science demands the recognition of two fundamental principles. The first one was perhaps best stated by Thomas Jefferson, who said, "I know of no safe depository of the ultimate powers of the society but the people themselves; and if we think them not enlightened enough to exercise their control with a wholesome discretion, the remedy is not to take it from them, but to inform their discretion." If the public is not adequately informed about a major issue, the government should not just go ahead and make the decision—instead, it must try to air the facts and the opposing views. (In the process, the government will probably learn something itself.) This leads somewhat to the second principle, that environmental safety is not merely an incomprehensible scientific notion, coldly objective and only definable by experts. Science must be able to be applied in the real world. Both of these principles illustrate the inescapable fact that successful environmental policy is based, at bottom, on an understanding of what is necessary and important for the government to accomplish.

EPA is in a good position to be able to meet these demands. We now have the capacity to have an almost contemporaneous running commentary on the environmental consequences of our society's technological developments. It certainly was not this way during the industrial revolution, or even during more recent periods in our history. Over the next several years, the public will become increasingly involved in the entire stream of policy development, including the role of science.

EPA's process of reformulating environmental policy, which was developed in response to these trends, is based on what I call "three pillars of change." The first pillar is strategic planning. Our experts need to step back and look at the relationship between the human activities that we regulate and their impact on natural systems and human health, and then make rough comparisons of the risks of exposure among the various kinds of stresses that humans impose on the environment. After this information comes in, policy makers must set priorities of what to act on first.

The second pillar is pollution prevention. EPA believes that industry should develop production processes that prevent pollution in the first place, and has made pollution prevention a foundation stone in its overall approach. A central provision of the Clean Air Act Amendments of 1990, for example, focuses on reducing risk by using market incentives and applying available technologies that are reasonably cost effective. Our Green Lights and 33/50 programs urge pollution prevention in a voluntary fashion in the areas of efficient lighting and toxic emissions reduction. Once government and industry have worked together to reduce our most critical forms of pollution in a cost-

The public will become increasingly involved in the entire stream of policy development.

effective manner—a process that has already started, and with dramatic results—we will be able to assess what risks remain, how they compare with each other, and how much we want to spend as a society to deal with them.

The third pillar of change is provided by Total Quality Environmental Management. We have established Total Quality throughout the agency, enabling our employees to focus on what excellence in environmental protection means. We are actively involving a broader spectrum of people at an earlier stage in investigation and policy development. This includes not only those who are working on the front lines of the developing policy within EPA, but also those outside the agency. Total Quality requires that EPA employees keep themselves open to ideas from others, see the big picture, and solve problems jointly. It also means that in solving problems we should never forget who our customers are and that we are striving for continual improvement. This inherently requires that we decide what the most important environmental risks are and act on them decisively.

Risk assessment is an elegant statement that EPA cannot be all things to all people. We must try to solve the most important problems first, and proceed on the basis of good science. A report released in 1990 by EPA's independent Science Advisory Board (*Reducing Risk: Setting Priorities and Strategies for Environmental Protection*) and a 1992 report on science at EPA that was authorized by a panel of experts have contributed greatly to EPA's vision of science and risk assessment. We are still in the process of translating these far-reaching recommendations into day-to-day policy, and the process—as with all cultural changes—will not be completed overnight. Quality risk assessment produces a tapestry of information that is both understandable and useful, with the threads woven in a way that allows us to see not only the gaps but also the picture that is taking shape. It will be challenging to consistently weave this tapestry in a scientifically reliable way. The credibility and understandability of the underlying risk assessments will be key to the agency's success.

While moving forward on these dramatic new fronts, building a foundation of quality and increased interaction on risk assessment, we at EPA are not changing our commitment to implementing and enforcing the existing environmental laws. It is sometimes difficult to operate under existing laws and regulations while remaining open to new developments in science. But that is exactly what we must do—good science and total quality environmental management demand it. Every day, EPA is involved in integrated activities where notions of comparative risk are crucial. We have been developing and issuing a series of state-of-the-art guidelines on a wide variety of risk assessments, including those relating to cancer exposure. We are institutionalizing early peer review and fair and thorough characterization of risk to ensure that we develop and maintain agency-wide consistency in exposure scenarios and provide up-to-date information to the public. Certainly, the most effective approach to environmental protection is one that merges all that is known about a problem with all that can be done to solve it. We must be aware of what is going on both inside and outside the agency, involve more people, and—wherever possible—get the scientists and policy makers on the same wavelength.

We all have a stake in the EPA's—and the whole government's—credibility in risk assessment. There are few things more disheartening to the citizens of a country than hearing constant criticism of the quality of the work done by the government or seeing with their own eyes the results of less than well conceived government projects. Environmental problems touch all lives. To effectively solve them, we must first focus our priorities and address the important environmental risks so that our limited resources are used for the benefit of all. Environmental policies that are based on this kind of thinking and on an inclusive process are precisely what give credibility to government action in this very important area.

F. Henry Habicht II is senior vice president at Safety-Kleen Corporation, an environmental company in Elgin, Illinois. At the time of the conference, he was deputy administrator of the Environmental Protection Agency.

Containing Violence by Containing Risk

• **RALPH NADER**

W E NEED TO MINIMIZE THE WORD RISK and use the word violence, because what we are talking about is the prevention and containment of violence, for example, chemical violence and genetic violence. We must always keep the empirical demonstration of violent effects in front of us so that we never forget what is at stake and do not become intellectually dishonest and incompetent.

What we call risk assessment is a movement toward massive overcomplication and overabstraction. Conventional cost-benefit risk assessment and comparative risk assessment are trying to make something precise which by the nature and number of all parties concerned cannot be precise. All parties will inject qualitative considerations that are never going to be quantified.

Conventional figures on the cost of safety regulation are typically arbitrary, using insupportable multiplier effects based on some constants that often have no relation to the cost to the economy. This threat of overmonetization of our social conscience and our social policies is evident in the politics of the Office of Management and Budget, which often results in policies driven by private contacts.

The key question here is, what is cost? The cost of bailing out the savings and loan industry, owing to its own speculation, mismanagement, and corruption, is not viewed as so serious a cost to the overall economy as when a fraction of that amount is applied to inconveniencing an industry to put it on a safer course of action. In fact, money spent on pollution control or safety advancement has a much better economic multiplier effect for economic growth than the enormous corporate welfare programs from Washington year in and year out.

People treat risks or hazards differently, depending on whether they are voluntary, involuntary, or addictive risks. People also treat risks that are offensive to their senses differently than risks that are not. Chemical risks

People treat risks or hazards differently, depending on whether they are voluntary, involuntary, or addictive risks.

frighten people because they can be hazardous without hurting anybody immediately. Radiation is another example. When people do not have sensory defenses against a peril, they have to have trust. People are expected to trust the government and the company that say things are okay. But how can people have trust after years of inaction by these officials and executives? Experts must take their intellectual system and put it in the minds of people who have different personal exposures to risks and see how that intellectual system changes—to see whether it is made more rigorous, more humane, or is discarded as being unworthy of the description.

The use of risk assessment in politics is subject to all of the prejudices (economic, social, racial) that afflict any policy. If we make a list of the traumas or diseases that are overwhelmingly in need of applying long-known measures or treatments, we will see that we are not dealing with them because we lack knowledge or probabilities or anything else, but because we lack willpower, courage, mobilization, priorities. For example, food piles up in government warehouses while millions of children worldwide are grossly undernourished. This violence needs to be prevented or reduced greatly. It has very little to do with the need for better risk assessment but everything to do with the need for government and other institutions to do the jobs that have been given to them.

The perpetuation of hazards is the outcome of the old problems of greed, power, cowardice, profiteering, institutionalized arrogance, and so on. William Haddon, who pioneered accident-injury prevention and treatment analysis, did not follow the usual risk assessment pattern. Instead, he talked in terms of strategies—reducing damage from hazards of all kinds—that can be applied in many areas. These strategies are: prevent the creation of the hazard; reduce the amount of the hazard being introduced; prevent the release of the existing hazard; modify the rate of spatial distribution of release of the hazard from its source; separate in time or in space the hazard and the people to be protected; separate the hazard from the people to be protected by interposition of a material barrier; modify relevant basic qualities of the hazard itself; make that which is to be protected more resistant to damage from the hazard; and stabilize, repair, and rehabilitate the object of the damage. Rather than concentrating on rigged risk cost-benefit and cost-effectiveness, we should work on the relative frequencies of specific kinds of damage, together with their imposed costs, and we can set priorities accordingly. This approach forces a full consideration of factors that can be commonly and cheaply applied, with far more satisfactory results.

If we look at the greenhouse effect, we could say that it really does not justify spending billions of dollars today because it really is not doing any damage now. But we know that if we do not do anything about it now, its damage could be catastrophic 100 years from now. The same retrospective view can be applied with cigarette smoking. How could we have justified doing anything about cigarette smoking in the 1920s based on what was known then in terms of any cost-benefit analysis? It is very easy to wait for the ever more refined risk assessment and to get detoured in that area at the expense of doing the job today, that is, to control or prevent the violence. We really should begin to focus on the enormous arrears of known hazards that are killing, injuring, and sickening people every day, such as tuberculosis, for which we have established rational measures of prevention or treatment.

Ralph Nader is a consumer advocate based in Washington, D.C.

PART 2

The Role of Federal Agencies in Regulating Risk

INTRODUCTION BY THOMAS A. BURKE

R isk assessment, as we currently practice and apply it, is at an important crossroads. As the need for improving the scientific basis for regulatory decisions increases, so it seems do the questions and doubts about risk assessment. As the political debates over regulatory approaches have escalated, so too has the gap between public perceptions and scientific estimates of risk.

The following two quotes from *Science* magazine underscore the scientific and social debate that faces today's risk manager. The first concerns hazardous waste cleanup:

> If current ill-based regulatory levels continue to be imposed, the costs of cleaning up hazards will be in the hundreds of billions of dollars, with minimal benefits to human health. In the meantime, real hazards are not receiving adequate attention. [P. H. Abelson, vol. 249 (1990)]

The second regards regulatory approaches to asbestos:

> To those of us who have spent our lives in public health research, it seems strange and sad that a country with one of the highest infant mortality rates in the western world and no shortage of other health and behavioral problems should commit billions of dollars to the questionable control of a minuscule or non-existent health risk. Perhaps the real problems are too difficult. [J. C. McDonald and A. D. McDonald, vol. 249 (1990)]

The general public, fueled by mixed messages and an erosion of trust in government, is increasingly frustrated.

These powerful statements underscore the challenge facing today's risk manager. It has become common for members of the scientific community to say that risk regulations are missing the mark. Industry often claims that the regulators have gone too far with costly approaches to insignificant risks. At the same time, there is increasing frustration on the part of the general public, which is fueled by these mixed messages and an erosion of trust in government.

Decision making amidst the conflicts of public outrage, competing budget priorities, and scientific uncertainty is often a thankless, but nonetheless essential, task. The need for refining the scientific process is essential. So too, however, is the need to integrate public values more effectively into the risk characterization process. The lines drawn in the 1983 National Academy of Sciences' "Red Book" have become blurred, particularly the dotted line between the risk assessor and the risk manager.

In this panel we hear from representatives of four agencies that must walk the line between risk assessment and risk management in assessing and regulating four distinct types of risks. We will also hear from the Office of Management and Budget, which, representing the Executive Office of the President, is charged with reviewing the regulatory approaches of these agencies and evaluating their costs.

Frederick Allen is the deputy director of the Environmental Protection Agency's Science, Economic, and Statistics Division. EPA has been the national leader in the use of comparative risk approaches to guide regulatory priorities. Mr. Allen's presentation provides an overview of the comparative risk approach, with an emphasis on the importance of integrating public values into the decision-making process.

Charles Adkins is director of Health Standards Programs at the Occupational Safety and Health Administration. OSHA has been the focal point in the national debate on risk regulation. In his presentation, Dr. Adkins describes the agency's approach to balancing risks and the role courts have played in shaping that approach.

Steven Luchter of the Department of Transportation, National Highway Traffic Safety Administration, provides a vivid contrast to quantitative risk assessment in his description of the DOT approach to measuring and preventing transportation risks.

Fred Shank of the Food and Drug Administration's Center for Food Safety provides a view of that agency's approach to managing risks in the food supply. His presentation includes an examination of the way in which the Delaney Clause of the Food, Drug and Cosmetic Act has shaped FDA's approach to regulating carcinogenic risks.

Finally, Richard Belzer of the Office of Information and Regulatory Affairs describes the oversight role of the OMB. His presentation offers insights into the process of reviewing agency regulations, and attempts to evaluate the basis for regulations, cost effectiveness, and benefits of regulatory programs.

Thomas A. Burke, Ph.D., M.P.H., is an assistant professor in the Department of Health Policy and Management, Johns Hopkins University School of Hygiene and Public Health.

Environmental Protection Agency

• FREDERICK W. ALLEN

T HERE ARE A LOT OF ENVIRONMENTAL PROBLEMS, and they cannot all be the most important. The key questions should be: What is the most important, and what do the people want?

When the public is asked to rank environmental risks, the dramatic, sensational, dreaded, well-publicized problems are at the top of their list. The more familiar, accepted causes that claim lives are down at the bottom. For example, while radon has been ranked by the Environmental Protection Agency as a more serious problem than hazardous waste, the public ranked hazardous waste at the very top and radon near the bottom of their list. (See Table 1 for a summary of the Roper report on *What the Public Wants.*)

EPA Administrator William Reilly, concerned with what our priorities should be, turned to the EPA's Science Advisory Board (SAB) and asked them to review the EPA's 1987 *Unfinished Business* report that compared the risks of all the different environmental problems. The result of his request was a report titled *Reducing Risk: Setting Priorities and Strategies for Environmental Protection.* This report looked at a wide range of risk data on all the different environmental problems and came up with a few conclusions on ranking and recommendations. The first recommendation was that the EPA ought to target its environmental protection efforts on the basis of the greatest opportunities for risk reduction. Other recommendations concerned working risk issues into the budget and planning processes, as well as other related subjects. In response to a point made earlier in this conference, one thing the report did not do was to recommend that a wall be put up between risk managers and the public.

Comparative risk is full of uncertainties and professional judgment, but it is a way of ordering what we know and the information we have. It should be introduced into the public debate with all the caveats in order to inform that debate. Risk is not the only factor that should be factored into priority setting.

Should a democracy focus its resources
where it can have
the greatest impact on health and welfare
or on those problems
about which the public is most upset?

Laws, economics, technology, the current state of agency programs, the benefits of the activities causing the risks, and public opinion must all be considered.

The uncertainties about comparative risk analysis are often not as important as they might seem at first. Moreover, because of the multiple factors, there is no magic formula that one can devise to set priorities. Every environmental problem has its own unique aspects that must become the subject of value judgments. That is why, in our system of government, elected members of Congress and presidential appointees who are confirmed by the Senate are the ones who make judgments on priorities. Public policy makers and all those involved in discussing environmental problems and risks need to recognize how the public may react to problems and risks, to understand why the risks have been assessed technically as high or low, and to tailor policies and communications to accommodate differing perspectives. Experts need to avoid thinking of the public as wrong or irrational when, in fact, the public may simply be using a different rationale.

The difference between public rankings and expert rankings raise an important issue for a democracy. Should a democracy focus its available resources and technology where it can have the greatest tangible impact on human and ecological health and welfare, or should it focus them on those problems about which the public is most upset? What is the proper balance? Our challenge is to bring the two viewpoints closer together. This is the most important challenge for risk communication.

Table 1. Environmental protection in the 1990s:

What the public wants *

1. The mandate for environmental protection is strong and getting stronger.

   The public's environmental agenda is broadening . . . more problems are being added; few are being removed . . .the situation is not under control.

2. Business is seen as largely responsible for environmental problems, but there is little sense that business is responding . . . or can be trusted.

3. Therefore, the public strongly favors government regulatory efforts.

4. Changes in public behavior lag far behind changes in attitude . . . but there are . . . signs of change.

5. There is not a single American "public" when it comes to the environment many shades of green . . . a need to segment.

ISSUES FOR CONSIDERATION:

1. The importance of language

2. Are we becoming a divided society regarding the environment?

3. A change in orientation to focus on ecological risk runs counter to the perspective of most Americans . . . the need must be "sold."

---

* A presentation to the EPA June 1991 by the Roper Organization, Inc.

Frederick W. Allen is acting director of the Science, Economics and Statistics Division, Office of Policy, Planning and Evaluation, Environmental Protection Agency.

Occupational Safety and Health Administration

• CHARLES E. ADKINS

OSHA HAS MADE SEVERAL ADJUSTMENTS in its regulatory process since its founding in 1971. Some adjustments have been self-initiated whereas others have been legally mandated. In the early 1970s, OSHA's regulatory process was based on scientific evidence that qualitatively established the existence of a hazard. Within this premise, OSHA's approach to control exposure to carcinogens was to set a permissible exposure limit as low as could feasibly be reached. The benzene standard was legally challenged on the basis that OSHA needed to demonstrate substantial benefits based on cost-benefit analysis. The same issue was later revisited in court with the cotton dust standard.

In the cotton dust case, the Supreme Court ruled that OSHA's standards were not to be based on cost-benefit analysis but must consider both the cost and the benefit of the standards. In the benzene decision, the Court held that before OSHA issued a new standard, it must determine that a significant risk exists and that the risk be based on quantitative estimates. The Court stated that it is the agency's responsibility to determine what is considered a significant risk. The Court also indicated that a significant risk determination was not a mathematical straitjacket, that OSHA is not required to support its findings with anything approaching scientific certainty, that review courts should give OSHA some leeway where its findings must be made on the frontiers of scientific knowledge, and that the agency is free to use conservative assumptions in interpreting the data with respect to carcinogens, risking error on the side of overprotection rather than underprotection.

Since then, OSHA has used the quantitative risk assessment method. In determining the desired level, OSHA has tried to reach the risk level of one in 1000 or less, as suggested by the Supreme Court. In most cases, this has not been done owing to the infeasibility of reaching an exposure level that would reduce the risk to this level. In those cases, OSHA has set a limit based on engineering feasibility and indicated that a residual significant risk remains at that level.

This is not an acceptable way to operate. We should not be satisfied with a significant residual risk if there is a means to reduce risk. Establishing exposure limits based on engineering controls alone means that we are not doing our best to prevent occupational risk. We must determine a method that will establish a level that is acceptable from a risk standpoint, and then determine the approach to be used to reach this level. This could lead to a two-tiered approach in which we establish a risk level and a separate engineering feasibility level.

Traditional risk assessment is based on exposure to a material without consideration of any other factors. OSHA's comprehensive standard typically contains components such as monitoring, medical surveillance, training, and personal protective equipment. These ancillary provisions have a tendency to reduce risk and should be taken into consideration.

OSHA's risk assessment consists of a critical evaluation of the data, a dose-response assessment to include low-dose effects, conversion from animal to human data and observed risk as demonstrated by epidemiological studies, and characterization of that risk. Each case is compared with the activities of other agencies, and differences are reviewed. In all cases, we carefully review the quality of the underlying data, the reasonableness of the risk assessment, the statistical significance of the findings, the type of risk presented, and the significance of numerical risks related to other risk factors.

Charles E. Adkins, C.I.H., is director of the Health Standards Program, Occupational Safety and Health Administration.

Office of Management and Budget

• Richard B. Belzer

T HE OFFICE OF MANAGEMENT AND BUDGET serves as the president's agent to ensure that regulatory actions are consistent with the president's regulatory principles. It reviews more than 2000 regulations each year, approximately 75 of which are classified as major (generally those that have economic consequences exceeding $100 million per year). Many of these regulations are aimed at reducing health and safety risks. A regulatory impact analysis must be prepared for each major regulation. OMB provides a convenient and potentially effective point within the Executive Office of the President for seeking consistency in risk regulation across federal agencies.

OMB's approach to regulatory policy is grounded in the principles of welfare economics. In the absence of a market failure, individuals are presumed to be the best arbiters of their own welfare, and they should be free to make their own decisions concerning the risks they take. When, however, significant market failures exist that inhibit or prevent efficient risk taking and risk avoidance, government may be an effective agent in restoring efficient market performance where markets are imperfect or in simulating efficient market performance where markets do not exist. Whether government intervention is warranted often depends on whether imperfect government programs and regulations are less distorting than the market failures they are intended to solve.

In this context, the purpose of government intervention is to achieve efficient risk taking and risk bearing, not necessarily to reduce risk. Risk is not always bad, and it cannot be eradicated from the face of the earth.

The principles that govern OMB's perspective toward risk can be found in Executive Order 12291, which directs federal agencies and departments to adhere to certain principles. First, regulatory action should be based on adequate information concerning the nature of a risk and some

Regulations aimed at reducing environmental and occupational cancer risks have extraordinarily high cost-effectiveness ratios.

notion that the proposed action will actually ameliorate it. Second, regulatory policies should focus on making regulations cost effective. Third, regulations should offer more risk reduction benefits to society than they cost in terms of lost social welfare.

We are concerned about risk assessment and risk management primarily because we have observed that the coercive powers of the federal government appear to be misallocated. My colleague John Morrall showed, in a study published in 1986, that there was tremendous variation in the cost effectiveness of federal regulatory proposals. The costs to avert a premature death ranged from less than $100,000 to $72 billion, a spread that has since increased. The upper bound is now no less than $5.7 trillion per premature death averted, which is roughly equivalent to the gross domestic product of the United States.

The absolute size of a risk is not a good indicator of whether government regulation is likely to be worthwhile. De minimis risks are sometimes very inexpensive to eliminate, whereas some very large risks cannot be reduced at any reasonable cost. Nevertheless, it is true that the regulations with the worst cost-effectiveness ratios tend to be aimed at very small risks.

Regulations aimed at improving transportation safety generally achieve cost-effective risk reduction. Regulations aimed at reducing occupational safety risks also tend to be cost effective. Regulations aimed at reducing environmental and occupational cancer risks, however, have extraordinarily high cost-effectiveness ratios, and they have been getting worse over time (see Figure 1).

Those who advocate more and more government intervention to re-

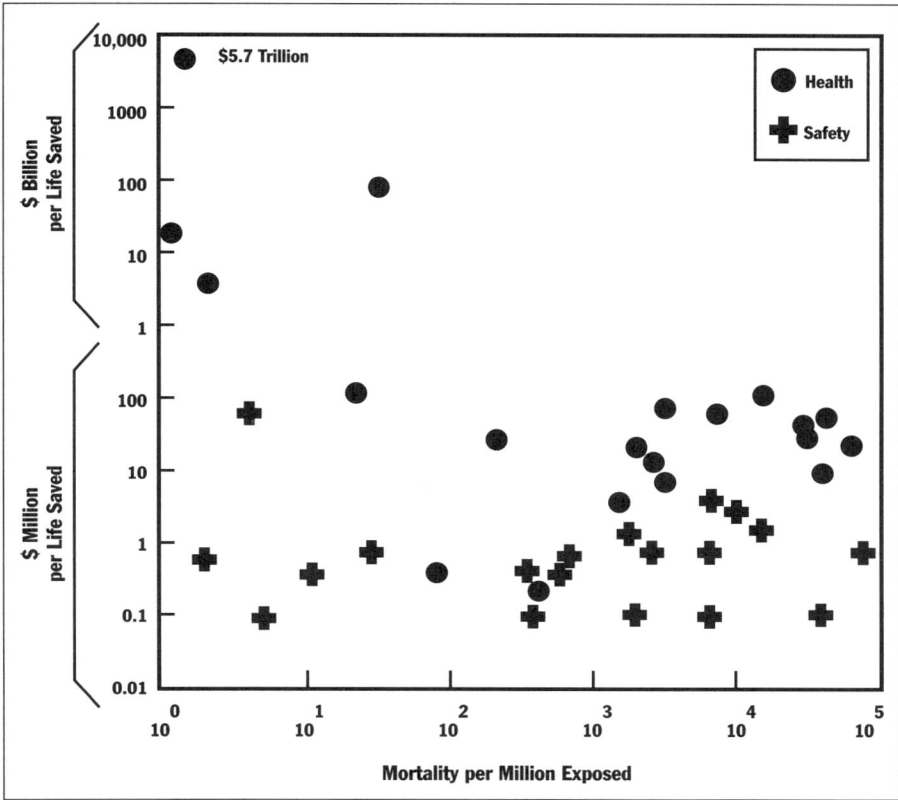

Mortality per Million Exposed

Legend:
- ● Health
- ✚ Safety

duce risk must face the economic implications of these actions. Are the gains from reducing risks really worth these enormous expenditures of scarce societal resources?

Richard B. Belzer, Ph.D., is an economist in the Office of Information and Regulatory Affairs, Office of Management and Budget. The views expressed are Dr. Belzer's and do not necessarily reflect the views of OMB.

Department of Transportation

• STEPHEN LUCHTER

RISK MEASUREMENT IN THE TRANSPORTATION SECTOR is focused primarily on fatalities. However, due to the large number of non-fatal injuries, particularly in motor vehicle crashes, methods have been developed to determine risks related to injuries, especially those that have long-term consequences.

There are five different levels of safety in transportation. The safest modes have risks lower than 0.1 fatalities per 100 million passenger miles. These include all bus, rail, and commercial aviation. A common characteristic of this category is that vehicle operation and maintenance are performed by professionals. The next modes have risks between 0.1 and 1.0, which include passenger cars, trucks, and commuter aviation. For the bulk of passenger cars and light trucks, individuals are responsible for operation and maintenance. The largest jump in risk appears in the light aircraft category, with risks between 1 and 10 fatalities per 100 million passenger miles. The least safe modes, which include motorcycles and bicycles (basically unenclosed vehicles), have more than 10 fatalities per 100 million passenger miles. Pedestrian transportation is the least safe means of travel.

Society appears to view risks of the various transportation modes very differently. We appear to be very sensitive to risk in transportation modes where we are not in control, despite the likelihood that the professionals who are in control are more competent. We also tend to underestimate the risk in modes where we are in control, apparently believing we are better-than-average operators. Also, we tend to be more risk tolerant in sports-type modes, where a little danger adds to the thrill. That may well be why motorcycle fatalities are as high as they are. We also tolerate fairly high risk in pedestrian and bicycle travel.

Quantifying risk of injury requires more than just a count of the number of people injured. The cost of injuries is also of interest. There are several ways to measure cost. Human capital costs include medical costs, productivity losses, property damage, legal and court costs, emergency costs, insurance and administrative expenses, and the cost of time lost by others in the traffic stream. These are essentially marketplace-oriented measures and relate to the gross national product. The costs of motor vehicle injuries and fatalities are the equivalent of about 2 percent of the gross national product.

Another way of measuring cost is called willingness to pay, which is a measure of what people are willing to pay to reduce the probability of an injury or fatality by a small amount. There are also ways other than cost to estimate the relative risk of various injuries. One of the methods is called the functional capacity index, which is an attempt to measure the reduction of the injured person's functional capacity during his or her remaining lifetime. It's a noneconomic approach for assessing the significance of injuries and fatalities.

The Department of Transportation, thus, is aware of risk measurement but does it differently than other governmental departments do. In short, DOT uses risk measurement to determine which countermeasures are cost effective or cost beneficial. It has developed a number of methods to do so, and is continuing this development.

Stephen Luchter is chief of Planning and Policy Development, National Highway Traffic Safety Administration, Department of Transportation.

Food and Drug Adminstration

• FRED R. SHANK

THE FOOD AND DRUG ADMINISTRATION regulates not only to assure the safety of food but also to provide standards of food identity designed to minimize fraud and adulteration. Food regulation is complex not only because food itself is complex but also because food has become an emotional issue. If and when there is a perception of a threat to the quality or safety of any item in the food supply, the public often responds with an outcry.

Scientific data that show the presence or absence of hazard form the basis of FDA regulations. In most cases, safety standards for food additives are based on the legal definition of safety, which means that there is a reasonable certainty in the minds of competent scientists that the substance is not harmful under the intended conditions of use. The agency tests most substances by animal bioassays. Typically, the highest level at which the substance has no observed effect on the animal is determined and then divided by 100 to arrive at a level that is considered to be safe for human consumption.

The 1958 food additive amendments, including the so-called Delaney Clause, specifically require demonstration of safety and prohibit the use of any carcinogenic substances in food. For substances that are themselves not carcinogenic but may contain carcinogenic impurities, the FDA developed a carcinogenic constituents or impurities policy that allows for an assessment of cancer risk. The assessment requires information on both exposure and carcinogenic potency from which the agency calculates an upper estimate of lifetime risk for a specific impurity from a particular use of the substance.

Since 1982, the agency has used the constituents policy in issuing more than 50 regulations. The use of risk assessment has allowed the agency to make decisions that both ensure protection of the public health and permit the use of substances that may contain insignificant amounts of carcinogenic impurities. The risk assessments, however, are not always straightforward nor do they always involve carcinogenic effects. The agency manages them on a case-by-case basis. Cases can be as simple as the contamination of a food, or food contact products, with lead, or as complex as that of aflatoxin affecting corn and peanuts.

In the case of lead, because toxicity is well known, there is no argument against the minimization or cessation of exposure to lead. If, hypothetically, lead were intentionally added to the food supply as a component, the agency would set criteria for this addition based on its worst-case exposure assessments. In the case of aflatoxin, the substance is not intentionally added to food and to some extent is unavoidable. To prevent all carcinogenic risk from exposure to aflatoxin, we need to set a zero tolerance for it in all crops. The law, however, does not require that there be zero tolerance because it is almost impossible to completely avoid aflatoxin on all grains. The agency therefore developed a tolerance based on a risk level that would minimize the risk yet allow potentially affected crops to be a part of the food supply.

In the case of saccharin, the FDA proposed banning the compound based on the Delaney Clause and on early studies of its carcinogenic effects. Congress, however, later enacted the Saccharin Study and Labelling Act, which imposed a moratorium on the agency's action. Data now indicate that saccharin is roughly 10 million times less carcinogenic than aflatoxin. From a scientist's perspective, the Delaney statute did not provide for scientific judgment in the decision-making process.

We need to consider either changing the Delaney Clause or allowing for greater latitude, discretion, and judgment in Delaney-based risk decisions. However, it can be changed only by Congress or by the insistence of the public wanting it to be changed. Until the statute changes, the FDA must continue to base regulations on the existing law. It is the agency's desire to be in a position to consider regulation of food safety based upon risk assessments. Additionally, the FDA must draw from and improve upon its ability to communicate with the public.

Fred R. Shank, Ph.D., is director of the Center for Food Safety and Applied Nutrition, Food and Drug Administration.

PART 3

The Role of Science in Understanding Risk: Limits and Opportunities

INTRODUCTION BY CAROL J. HENRY

Risk assessment—the characterization of the probability of potentially adverse health effects from human exposures to environmental hazards—is, and will continue to be, an imprecise science. It is, however, the only means we have of trying to assess quantitatively the potential adverse effects of many useful, and even essential, substances on human health. Thus, at the same time we are forced to acknowledge the limits of risk assessment, we must work to decrease the uncertainties inherent in the process by improving the science on which risk assessments are based. As well, we must make better use of the scientific information we now have to manage risks more effectively.

I can cite several areas where I believe we should be concentrating our scientific resources to improve risk assessment. First, we must acquire more data on the true extent of human exposure to potentially harmful substances. Using this information, we need to design animal studies to investigate how these exposures may or may not result in adverse health effects in humans—not just carcinogenic effects, but reproductive, developmental,

Priorities must be created so that chemicals with the greatest potential for harm are investigated and those with inadequate data are not ignored.

and neurotoxic effects as well.

Second, it is essential that we improve our understanding of the mechanisms of action of harmful substances. Recognizing the importance of this, the National Toxicology Program has begun to reorganize its bioassay program to examine underlying mechanisms of toxicity that will enhance our understanding of the biologic activity of the substances being tested. Precisely what is going on at the molecular and the genetic levels to cause adverse effects observed in experimental animals? When can we—and when can we not—assume that the same mechanistic explanations that account for adverse changes in experimental animals can be applied to human exposures? In the absence of information, it is prudent public health policy to assume that events in animal bioassays—systematic studies of the effects of certain compounds on experimental animals over the lifetime or over generations—reflect potential activity in humans.

Third, we must make better use of chemical-specific data. We now have extensive data on some compounds but very little on others. The biological activity of some classes of chemicals is much better understood than that of others. Priorities must be created with which to conduct bioassays so that those chemicals with the greatest potential for harm are investigated and those with inadequate data are not ignored.

Fourth, we must take a stronger stance for prevention in order to reduce or prevent exposures to potentially harmful chemicals in the first place. While this makes sense intuitively, policies to date have emphasized not prevention but, instead, treatment and mitigation, generally a far more costly

We must develop
better scientific procedures
to help us predict which chemicals
are likely to present true risks to humans.

approach to dealing with harmful substances. To assist us in taking a preventive approach, we must develop better scientific procedures to help us predict which chemicals are likely to present true risks to humans. Likewise, we need to refine our testing procedures to improve our confidence that the hazards we identify do indeed present true risks for humans. We cannot afford false-positive or false-negative predictions or test results when we are dealing with human and environmental health.

Fifth, much work remains to be done in assessing what the relevance of data from laboratory animals is to human health. I needn't emphasize the enormous uncertainties of extrapolating from observations of adverse effects in laboratory animals exposed to high doses of substances down to the possible effects on humans of the generally minute levels to which they are likely to be exposed. We can and will find ways to eliminate some of the uncertainty. Will compounds that produce lesions in the organs of experimental animals—the so-called target organs—affect the same organs in humans? Will they affect different organs? Are physiologically based pharmacokinetic data—information on the means by which and rate at which compounds are absorbed and eventually eliminated by the body—from high-dose animal studies applicable to humans at the low doses to which they are likely to be exposed?

Because the need for more scientific data to improve the risk assessment process is virtually unlimited, it is essential to create priorities. This will require greater dialogue with risk managers, the professionals charged with reducing or eliminating risks from the workplace and the larger environment or with establishing acceptable trade-offs for essential compounds that carry a measure of risk to human health and well-being. What information do risk managers need from risk scientists to do their job? Does compound A present more of a risk than compound B at the worksite? Does compound C present a risk to experimental animals that, because of the mechanism of action or route of exposure, is likely to cause no harm in humans?

The need for skilled communication between risk scientists and risk managers, who are often not scientists, cannot be overemphasized. How can risk scientists communicate their data and information effectively to risk managers? And how, in turn, can risk managers communicate with their constituents—workers, government officials, and the general public—to assure them that substances of proven benefit to human beings do not also carry unacceptable risks to health and well-being?

It is inevitable that the role of science in understanding and managing risk will grow. It is up to those of us who are involved in risk assessment, management, and communication to see that this growth is targeted wisely to eliminate as much uncertainty as we can from the risk assessment process. Armed with better data, risk scientists must help the risk manager reduce or eliminate as much exposure as possible from the workplace, the home, and the larger environment.

I have given you an overview of what I think some of the "mega-issues" are in risk science today. In the presentations that follow, three eminent risk scientists will give you their perspectives on the role of science in understanding risk.

Carol J. Henry, Ph.D., is director of the Office of Environmental Health Hazard Assessment, California Environmental Protection Agency. At the time of the conference, she was executive director of the ILSI (International Life Sciences Institute) Risk Science Institute.

The Shift to Exposure Data

• BERNARD D. GOLDSTEIN

THIS CONFERENCE IS SUBTITLED "The Science and Politics of Risk," but there is almost no science. It is really a risk management meeting because we are talking to an audience that deals with risk management, politics, and communications. The confusion reflected in the title, unfortunately, extends to the field of risk assessment. Much of the criticism of risk assessment relates not to the science on which it is based, but to policy judgments that are incorporated into the risk assessment process.

If we agree that we are doing a reasonable job of estimating risks, what will more science get us? If the science can inform the process in terms of dose-response estimations, we should be getting less conservative as we get more science. This is because we are using upper-bound conservative approaches. Thus, decreasing the uncertainty in the dose-response estimation will more often than not decrease the risk.

It is the opposite on the hazard identification side: by doing research we are more likely to find hazards we did not expect. The story of lead toxicity is one of increasing regulation after research. Through research, we found that lead is toxic at even lower levels than previously thought. Based on new scientific evidence, we were able to decide that we needed more stringent regulation.

To understand quantitative risk assessment, it is important to understand what the data quality objective is. This has to do with how precise we expect our endpoint to be. There is a big difference between the relatively broad data quality objective of the risk scientist and what the risk manager has used, or been forced to use by pressure of public events, as a data quality objective. A "bright line" based on a risk of one in 1 million is a data quality objective inconsistent with our scientific understanding of risk assessment measurement. There needs to be a better translation of the scientist's data quality objective into what it is that the risk manager needs to know, and vice versa.

Another important limitation of risk assessment is its inability to be fully a priority-setting process. The most important thing that the Environmental Protection Agency and other federal agencies have done in terms of chemical risk is the primary preventive approach, that is, not letting the chemical get manufactured or distributed in the first place. It is very difficult, nonetheless, to quantitate risks that have not yet occurred. If we are forced to focus on existing problems and forget about primary prevention, we will have distorted the process in such a way that we will always fall behind.

In the new Clean Air Act, Congress appears to have decided not to be concerned about risk because it is too complicated. The act treats all chemicals equally in the first go-round of technology-based controls, after which risk assessment would occur. There is an apparent lack of understanding of the differences in risk for different chemicals.

A good feature of the Clean Air Act is that it should lead to more emphasis on exposure assessment. Most of the debates about risk assessment of individual chemicals have been on the hazard side, but we know relatively little about the extent of human or ecosystem exposure. There is so much we could learn in this area, and the opportunity for improving risk science is great. We will find more and more exposure work being done, and this is where the future debates will reside.

Whether the major focus is on the politics of risk policy or the management of risk, the exclusion of science from the policy and process of risk assessment is such that perhaps we need to refocus our thinking on the scientific basis of risk assessment.

Bernard D. Goldstein is director of the Environmental and Occupational Health Sciences Institute, a joint program of the University of Medicine and Dentistry of New Jersey—Robert Wood Johnson Medical School and Rutgers University.

Risk Managers Need More and Better Data

• JOSEPH V. RODRICKS

A GREAT DEAL OF SCIENTIFIC INFORMATION available to the risk assessor often plays little or no role in the ultimate decision about regulation of particular risks or sources of risks. The quality and quantity of data available to the risk assessor vary greatly among different chemicals. For example, the database for some substances that are labeled carcinogens may be fairly limited, including only a single study of a substance's carcinogenicity and some data on short-term toxicity, and perhaps some investigations into its capacity to damage genetic material. At the other extreme, the database for some carcinogens may include several long-term cancer studies, and there may even be available one or more epidemiological investigations. Most other carcinogenic substances are characterized by databases that fall between these two extremes.

The current regulatory approach would tend to disguise these substantial database differences and focus on the specific sets of data, together with the needed science policy assumptions, that lead to what regulators call an upper-bound estimate of risk. Regulatory risk assessments may contain substantial discussions of the database, but the final risk characterization generally relies on the specific sets of data and assumptions that yield this so-called upper-bound estimate. Under this regulatory practice, database differences and their possible implications for human risk are hidden. The risk manager is not afforded a complete sense of the relative complexities and uncertainties in the data available for different regulated substances.

An alternative model for the risk assessment process is one in which the risk assessor has a more restricted, albeit more difficult, role, and a larger role is given to the risk manager. In this proposed model, the risk assessor's job is not to make the ultimate judgment on which of several possible sets of data and assumptions are to be used in the characterization of risk. The risk assessor would instead be asked to explore and make explicit the implications for human risk of all available human, animal, and experimental data, including any related to the chemical's mechanisms of action. It is also the risk assessor's role to illustrate the relative scientific strengths and weaknesses—the uncertainties—associated with each of the several risk outcomes available for a given substance.

Under this model, the risk assessor is not making the policy decision to eliminate from consideration certain data sets or assumptions because they are "too uncertain"; rather, the assessor shows the implications for risk of all available data sets and plausible assumptions, describes their relative scientific merits, and leaves to the risk manager the ultimate decision about which estimate(s) will be relied upon for decision making.

It could be suggested that although the standard regulatory model provides the upper bound on risk, the use of alternative data sets and assumptions as proposed in this new model produces lower estimates of risk, and because they are uncertain, reliance on them could jeopardize human health. The use of several alternatives nevertheless creates an outcome that is more faithful to our true state of scientific understanding than one that is based on selected and limited sets of data and assumptions. Furthermore, faced with an array of information, the policy maker is in a position to develop a sense of the uncertainties in the assessment and thus can make a more fully informed decision. The differences in the database and degree of scientific understanding among different substances are made explicit and can be taken into account in the decision process. When faced with scientific uncertainty, the policy maker can always opt for the upper-bound estimate if the regulatory context calls for maximum risk avoidance regardless of cost. If, however, the regulatory context calls for balancing risk reduction against other benefits, a full range of values may be more useful in the evaluation. Moreover, some central tendency can always be considered.

Use of this alternative model should serve to reduce the scientific debate (because it relies on a wider range of data and assumptions) or shift it to the more productive one of weighing the relative merits of various approaches to risk assessment. It also places greater responsibility for ultimate policy decisions in the hands of the risk manager, where it should be.

Joseph V. Rodricks, Ph.D., is senior vice president of ENVIRON Corporation.

Understanding the Mechanisms of the Dose-Response Relationship

• ROGER O. McCLELLAN

THE STRUCTURALLY INTEGRATED APPROACH to risk assessment is embodied in the paradigm of source, exposure, dose, and response. Of critical concern is the linkage between exposure and response. An understanding of this linkage can best be obtained through insights into the mechanisms linking exposure and dose, and dose and response (see Figure 1).

Some of the debate concerning risk revolves around where the information comes from. Today we continue to have significant debates on the relationship between exposure and the health outcome from epidemiological studies. It also has become somewhat fashionable in some circles to decry the lack of congruence between the information from those epidemiological studies and studies in laboratory animals. There is also concern for extrapolation from observations at high levels of exposure and with high prevalence of disease to calculated very low levels of disease at low levels of exposure.

It is inappropriate to focus on these incongruencies, except when they lead us to focus on how we can improve our approaches to using data from other biological systems. As we look to a future-oriented approach for risk assessment, we need to look at what we can do in terms of evaluating the potential risks of new products, new drugs, and new consumer products that are going to be needed. In these situations human data on late-occurring responses such as cancer will not be available. Thus, animal data will play a central role in estimating potential human health risks.

Assessing human health risks in the absence of human data is a challenge. If we have available human data, we only have to look at exposure and response and simply link them. Of course, knowledge of the mechanism of action of the agent will be useful in understanding the relationship between exposure and risk, especially when extrapolating to potential risks

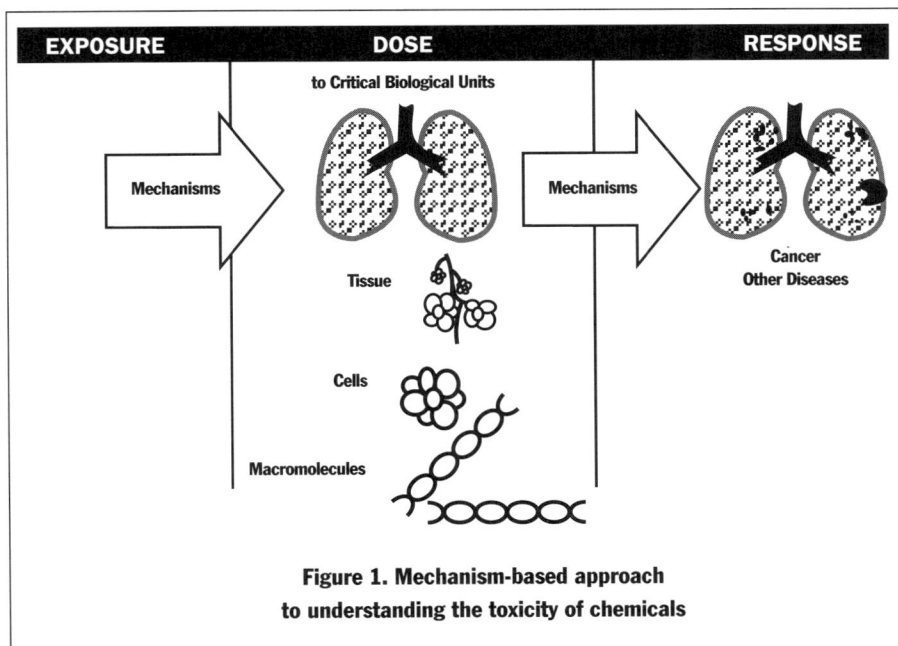

**Figure 1. Mechanism-based approach
to understanding the toxicity of chemicals**

at lower levels of exposure. The introduction of laboratory animal data, however, requires a substantial leap of faith if our approach to extrapolation from laboratory animals to man is based on the simple relationship of exposure to response alone. Here is where an understanding of the mechanisms that underlie those exposure-response relationships is critical. It is important to understand the extent to which the mechanisms operative in laboratory animals are likely to be operative in people.

It is no longer sufficient to say whether or not a material is a carcinogen or a reproductive toxin. We now want to know the potency of the material so that we can estimate the potential human health risks at relevant levels of exposure. Through an understanding of mechanistic data, we can develop a better understanding of the relevance of laboratory findings to man. This is the kind of mechanistic approach that we are going to have to take in the future as we deal with materials for which we have no human experience.

Our future challenge and opportunities are to understand the toxicity of chemicals and bring to bear on our risk assessment orientation an increasing ability to understand the mechanistic action of chemicals. With an emphasis

An understanding of the mechanisms
that underlie exposure-response relationships
is critical for understanding the relevance
of laboratory findings to man.

on the linkages between sources of materials, exposure, dose, and response, we can interpret, understand, and communicate the data.

We will need to continue to use data from a wide array of biological systems—the molecular level, the cell level, intact laboratory animals, and populations of laboratory animals—if we are going to adequately estimate human health risks. We also will likely need to continue to do these studies with high levels of exposure or large administered doses to maximize their sensitivity. This is going to further emphasize the need for a mechanistic orientation in order to understand the relevance of the findings at these levels and to be able to estimate human health risks at relevant levels of exposure. It is important to recognize that mechanisms of action may vary with level of exposure or dose, giving emphasis to the need to understand the likely mechanisms of action at relevant levels of exposure.

Roger O. McClellan, D.V.M., is president and chief executive officer of the Chemical Industry Institute of Toxicology.

PART 4

Risky Business: Improving Decision Making

INTRODUCTION BY FRED D. HOERGER

T his session focuses on how risk assessment and risk factors are integrated into the decision-making process and on the ultimate basis or rationale of final decisions. Three speakers will address the topic from the perspectives of an environmental organization, a regulatory agency, and an automobile manufacturing company. Collectively, the disciplinary background of the panelists includes expertise in toxicology, public health, regulatory policy analysis, and technical risk and social value analysis.

To state the obvious, decision making in the fields of health, safety, and the environment is a truly complex and value-laden endeavor, whether on a personal, institutional, or societal basis. Because of its multivalue nature, decision making by a government agency acting institutionally on behalf of society is truly risky business. Not all interested parties are likely to benefit; some are likely to be affected negatively. And decisions involve change in the status quo. Even those not directly affected may perceive unwanted trends and precedents.

Both what is regulated and how it is regulated are critical aspects of this risky societal endeavor. A whole plethora of choices surround priority setting. Many of the "what to regulate" decisions are resolved, deferred, or ambiguously side-stepped by Congress. Others are influenced by agency budgetary or administrative processes, by default, by petition, by public pressure and visibility, and by court mandates. The "how" of regulation involves another set of critical choices, such as risk-based standards, technology-based standards, market-based approaches, procedural and record-keeping requirements, information availability, and so on.

Although one might think that the background information and social value factors leading to the "what" and "how" decisions are quite different, practice seems to indicate that the differences are not substantive. Facts, estimates, and viewpoints relating to the extent or prevalence of risk, danger and disease, technological feasibility, costs, cost effectiveness, ethics, other social values, and ultimately political feasibility shape both the "what" and the "how" decisions.

The speakers focus on the factors that shape the "what" and "how" decisions. A number of key questions are addressed: Is the decision process working? What needs fixing or improving? How can risk assessment be improved? Can public health techniques for evaluation of disease and greater reliance on actuarial injury and mortality data improve decisions? The panelists provide unique and provocative insights into these questions.

Fred D. Hoerger, Ph.D., is retired from Dow Chemical Company, where, at the time of the conference, he was in the company's Health and Environmental Science Unit.

A Proposal for Overcoming Paralysis in Improving Risk Regulation

• Ellen K. Silbergeld

IN CONSIDERING THE QUESTION of improving decision making under risk assessment, it is probably fair to start by asking, Does it need improvement? Is it working? If it isn't working, how badly is it failing us at the present time? Are we doing enough? Are we doing the wrong things? Are we perhaps just doing too much, as the Office of Management and Budget sometimes suggests? Or even more fundamental, is our world truly risky?

I would like to answer the first question—Is the decision-making process related to regulating risk in need of improvement?—with a very simple yes. But in addressing the need for improvement, we are hampered by paralysis.

Why are we so paralyzed, and how can we overcome this paralysis? Whether you think we are doing too much, too little, or selecting the wrong risks, we are proceeding in an erroneous fashion of analysis, gathering the wrong data and ignoring the right data. I propose to acknowledge this as a fact, without discussing what sorts of decisions we should be making, and deal only with how to overcome paralysis.

To improve decision making itself, I would suggest the following eight prescriptions. First, we need to open the process. We can take a great deal of pride in many of our laws and processes that allow an enormous amount of public participation in decision making, particularly in the environmental and occupational health field. Over the last 10 years, however, we have seen the rise of an occult power, the OMB, whose deliberations are not open and are not part of the American tradition of due process and full participation of all parties at interest. We need to keep the process open and to resist all forces that would internalize and hide various critical parts of the analytic or regulatory process.

Second, we need to speed up the process. One of the classic symptoms of paralytic policy making in this country is the abysmal slowness involved in reaching any decision.

We need to embed
our risk reduction steps
in health promotion.

Third, we need to keep track of decisions that we do make, and we need to keep track of them in terms of evaluating their impacts. We don't know whether those few actions that we have managed to take over the past 15 years really have made much difference in the spheres in which they were intended to have an impact. We need to empower data-gathering agencies and instruments, such as the Agency for Toxic Substances and Disease Registry and the National Health and Nutrition Examination Survey, to be sensitive to the kinds of end-points we are trying to regulate and determine whether the sorts of actions we are taking really do have an impact on the problem.

Fourth, we need to embed our risk reduction steps in health promotion, broadly speaking. The Environmental Protection Agency's current risk reduction effort does not grow out of a tradition of disease prevention and health promotion and a deep and thoughtful dialogue with the medical and public health community. This strategic integration would help end the tyranny of competing goals. It is very easy, particularly in Washington, D.C., to talk about how we would help more undernourished babies if we didn't spend so much money regulating trichloroethylene. Outside Washington, D.C., it's less easy to make this argument. A dollar not spent on regulating air pollution is not going to go to underweight babies. So, unless we establish a rubric for decision making that is truly broad, let us not set up one goal to compete with the other, because we end up doing nothing for either.

Fifth, we must debunk economics. It is time to return economics to its proper function as a tool to accomplish goals and to remove it from center stage, where it attempts to define what those goals should be.

Sixth, we should avoid or treat with a great deal of suspicion all priority-setting exercises. We do not need to empanel more internal or external experts to evaluate and reevaluate priority setting for an agency or even for a nation.

Seventh, we must learn from the past. We should pay more attention to the rise of public health policy, occupational health, and preventive diseases in the industrialized world. Assessing the successes, dangers, and problems we have encountered over most of the 20th century might assist us in developing new strategies for the next century.

Eighth, we need to combine the dominant toxicological perspective of risk assessment with the public health perspective. The toxicological perspective has been driven by noble goals—primarily preventive goals—out of which has arisen a large superstructure of chemical testing and hazard evaluation. The inference or the assumption of this toxicological perspective is that by identifying the biological and toxicological properties of a chemical substance, one is not only characterizing its hazard but also somehow identifying it as a cause of human disease or injury.

The public health perspective is quite different. The public health perspective begins with an assessment of disease—an evaluation of the prevalence of disease and the health status of a population or a cohort under study. From the careful examination of that population—its conditions, its attributes, and factors related to its course of life and disease—an attempt can be made to deduce or elucidate causes of disease or abnormal or altered health status within that group. Based on that disease-driven identification of causes, an estimate might then be back-calculated to the risks of those factors.

This public health perspective would cause us to look very differently at what is going on in the American population. It might help to overcome some of the divisions that occur among us when we try to understand what is important and what actions we should be taking.

Ellen K. Silbergeld, Ph.D., is professor of epidemiology and preventive medicine and professor of toxicology, School of Medicine, University of Maryland at Baltimore.

Risk Assessment and the Regulatory Process

• Elizabeth Drye

A RANGE OF VIEWS EXISTS about whether risk assessment is a useful decision-making tool. Some would prefer abandoning risk assessment because of the uncertainties associated with it. In my view, risk assessment is a valuable decision tool, but the extent of its usefulness varies depending on the certainty of the risk assessment and decision context.

In some cases, risk assessment can dramatically improve a regulatory decision. This is particularly true where the main benefit of the regulation is cancer risk reduction and the reduction can be estimated with a relatively high degree of certainty. An example is the Environmental Protection Agency's proposed regulation to establish drinking water standards for four radionuclides. Decision makers set radionuclide standards based on cancer risk reduction estimates rather than technological feasibility, which turned out to be a more cost-effective regulatory approach.

In some decisions, however, risk assessment plays a less clear role. It typically will not provide a definitive basis for choosing among regulatory alternatives where risk reduction estimates are relatively uncertain and where risk reduction is only one of several anticipated benefits of the regulation. This is the case with the agency's municipal landfill rule. In contrast to the radionuclide rule, the cancer risk assessment for the landfill rule was relatively uncertain. Furthermore, the rule was expected to affect not only human cancer risk but human noncancer risk, ecological risk, property values, and the ease of siting new landfills.

The promise of risk assessment has been exaggerated. If we expect risk assessment to provide simple solutions to complex problems, it will fail us. It is best viewed as a tool that provides important input into multidimensional, value-laden decisions. We should expect that in many, but not all, cases it will improve our decisions notably. We can improve our current use of risk assessment in two ways:

1. We should improve the tool itself by incorporating new scientific information into health risk assessment models and improving methods for better estimating noncancer health risks and ecological risks.
2. We should recognize that better science will not answer science policy questions about how risk information should be used in decision making (in fact, it might make our risk management decisions more complex), and we should have a more focused debate about how risk assessment results should be used in the regulatory context.

Elizabeth Drye is a Congressional Fellow in the office of Sen. Joseph I. Lieberman. At the time of the conference, she was special assistant to the acting assistant administrator of the Office of Policy, Planning and Evaluation, Environmental Protection Agency.

The Cost of Reducing Risk

• Richard C. Schwing

ROM AN INDIVIDUAL STANDPOINT, there are two reasons for not doing everything possible to achieve immortality: time and financial constraints. Society faces similiar constraints. About a decade ago, the ethicists and humanists confronted these issues head on.

Joseph Fletcher wrote in 1979: "We shall always have to decide who should be treated and who should not, who shall die and who shall live." The same perspective applies to health and safety. In dealing with these concepts of ethics, economics, and morality, Fletcher coined the term "ethimetrics"—a label for applying statistical terms of amount and probability to macromoral problems, even down to such levels as allocating budgets. Since Fletcher's time, it has become more acceptable to mention dollars and lives in the same sentence.

Based on the dollars (or cost) per life saved for 53 regulations promulgated by eight federal agencies, we can see that the data cover a tremendous range—from $100,000 to more than $100 billion (see Figure 1). The programs that abate safety-related deaths are, on average, several thousand times more efficient than those that abate health-related deaths. Three other observations also emerge: existing policies trade longevity for substantial costs, policy efficiencies vary over a wide range, and replacement of inefficient with efficient policies could further extend the nation's longevity.

It is possible, however, for society to paralyze itself in a search for zero risk. For example, the least efficient program analyzed by the Office of Management and Budget costs $5.7 trillion per life saved (see Figure 1), a figure that exceeds the current U.S. GNP. Clearly, we cannot spend the whole GNP to save one life. It turns out that if you ignore the fact that we also value education, our homes, our mobility, the arts, and other indices of the quality of life, each life could claim a little over $2 million.

There are prejudices, filters, and visions we collectively bring to bear on issues like this. One group says, "How can you be so inefficient and wasteful?" while the other group says, "How can you let those people die?"

Programs that abate safety-related deaths are several thousand times more efficient than those that abate health-related deaths.

What are the visions that we have as we approach risk analysis when freedom and human nature are confounded with human tragedy? A great deal of insight can be obtained from Thomas Sowell's work *A Conflict of Vision.*[1] Sowell's two dominant visions, the "constrained" and the "unconstrained" (see Table 1), relate to the polarization that exists in risk analysis.

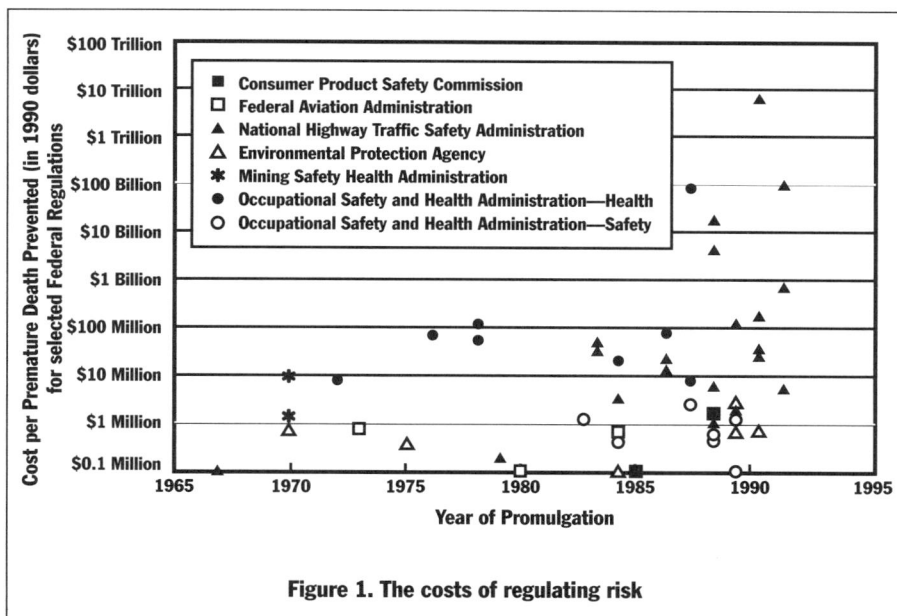

Figure 1. The costs of regulating risk

Note to Figure: Federal agencies include the Consumer Product Safety Commission, Mine Safety and Health Administration, Environmental Protection Agency, National Highway Traffic Safety Administration, Federal Aviation Administration, Federal Railroad Administration, Food and Drug Administration, and Occupational Safety and Health Administration (from U.S. Government, "Reforming Regulation and Managing Risk Reduction Sensibly," *Budget of the United States Government for Fiscal Year 1992* [Washington, D.C.: Government Printing Office, 1991], sec. IX.C, pt. 2, pp. 367-376.

Table 1: Insights relating to the existing polarization in risk analysis: a comparison of the unconstrained and constrained visions of life

UNCONSTRAINED	CONSTRAINED
Jean-Jacques Rousseau: Man is born free but everywhere he's in chains.	Thomas Hobbes: Life is solitary, poor, nasty, brutish, and short.
Voltaire Thomas Paine John Kenneth Galbraith Earl Warren	Adam Smith Alexander Hamilton Milton Friedman Oliver Wendell Holmes
What is desired? (a value-based premise)	What is achievable? (a fact-based premise)
Humans are perfectible.	Perfection is too costly to our humanity.
Institutions cure evil.	Institutions control evil.
Results, ends	Process, means
Society has not yet tapped the moral potential of humans.	Human defects are limiting, and we have limited and unhappy choices.
Solutions	Trade-offs
Clean and orderly	Messy and chaotic
Faith in the classroom	Faith in experience
Belief in models	Belief in data

Synthesized from Thomas Sowell, *A Conflict of Vision* (New York: William Morrow, 1986).

These views are predicated on the idea that "humans are perfectible" in the unconstrained view and that "perfection is too costly to our humanity" in the constrained view. Furthermore, the unconstrained can be characterized as taking the view that "institutions cure evil" versus the idea that "institutions control evil" in the view of the constrained. The unconstrained are motivated by results and ends, whereas the constrained focus on the process and the means. This difference in philosophies also leads to the notion of equality of results versus equality of opportunity.

Indeed, we are comparing an optimistic vision to a tragic vision of the world. The unconstrained seek a cause that is curable and accept people as people and merely try to control their behavior. They seek solutions that are clean and orderly. The constrained, by contrast, are satisfied with trade-offs that are messy and chaotic. Whereas the unconstrained have faith in the educational process and tend to believe in models when approaching problems, the constrained have more faith in experience and believe, most of all, in data. This dichotomy of the constrained and unconstrained represents the poles of many risk debates, especially in the debates of efficiency versus equity, the source of knowledge, and the role of models and analysis.

We are today enmeshed in a world that maintains both philosophies as credible, and risk management choices are embedded in both philosophies. Yet we cannot escape the constrained view when discussing health and safety priorities. When we look at the allocation of resources, we should be aware of the constrained and the unconstrained perspectives. As Sowell so aptly put it: "Everyone is part of the conflict of visions, and the stakes are as real as money, power, and, most important, survival."

---

[1] New York: William Morrow, 1986.

Richard C. Schwing, Ph.D., is principal research engineer in the Operating Sciences Department, General Motors Research and Development Center.

PART 5

Perceiving Risk: What Do People Worry About and Why?

INTRODUCTION BY JOHN F. AHEARNE

I n 1989, the National Academy Press published the report of the National Research Council Committee on Risk Perception and Communication, *Improving Risk Communication*. That report noted that "many participants in the [risk communication] process lack fundamental understanding of the important points that form the basis for successful risk communication". This panel addressed some of the fundamental issues regarding how people think about risk and explained some of the problems that agencies and institutions have in dealing with risk issues when in contact with the public.

The public's concerns often begin with the conclusion that risk is increasing. The National Research Council noted that "for many observers the central dispute about technology and risk concerns whether risk is increasing or decreasing" (p. 54). The committee noted that the two perspectives are that these are "the safest of times" (p. 55) or "the riskiest of times" (p. 56). Vincent Covello points out that although many in the public believe that most cancers in the United States are caused by chemical exposures, most scientists argue just the opposite, that most cancers are due to life-style factors. Cristine Russell also sees this as a major issue and notes that "a major technological paradox of our time is that it is both the riskiest and the

The difference in the ways that scientists and the public perceive and approach risk is fundamental to many of the conflicts in the public arena.

safest of times." She attributes this paradox to the difference in the way the public and experts view risk. The National Research Council identified a fundamental difference in the values that are at issue, and concluded that public disputes are often about "what kinds of risks people want most to avoid, what kinds of lives they want to lead, . . . and what the proper relationship is between humanity and nature" (p. 57). Therefore, as Russell points out, "the dispute cannot be resolved by available evidence."

This difference in the ways that scientists and the public perceive and approach risk is fundamental to many of the conflicts in the public arena. The messages of federal agencies and industry tend to be concerned with convincing the public that it should not worry. Covello and Russell illustrate through many examples why this is a faulty approach.

Differing perspectives on what risk is also often lead the technical community to not comprehend the intensity of the anger and the alienation felt by members of communities where environmental hazards have been identified. Michael Edelstein describes these as "environmental victims" and concludes that "outsiders simply do not understand environmental victimization." He pictures such "victims" as having lost any sense of control over their future, seeing their environment as dangerous, even their homes as unsafe. Viewing risk issues from this perspective, Edelstein concludes that "we need to recognize NIMBY [not in my back yard] as a legitimate reaction." It is unusual to see a defense of NIMBY by other than those persons who perceive themselves as directly at risk, but Edelstein describes this criticism of NIMBY as an illustration of misunderstanding of risk. Exacerbating the tension between the public and institutions is the lack of understanding of the public view on the part of institutional representatives. Therefore, their attempts at communicating often do not reflect those issues that the public is concerned about. Covello notes that "the lack of sensitivity to communication helps escalate the problem of public concern and hinders the ability to establish dialogue."

One of the conclusions of the National Research Council's study was that a common misconception among technologists is that the media are always a major source of problems between the public and institutions. Russell states that "the media certainly deserve a certain amount of blame for scaring the public with little perspective on what to worry about and what priorities are." However, while noting that "deadlines often leave little time to seek the big picture," she states that "much of the blame for the haphazard and confusing stories about risk in the media must be shared by the scientists and technical people, their institutions, the politicians, the government bureaucrats, and the competing industry and advocacy groups, all of whom often have axes to grind for a particular purpose." That same conclusion was reached by the National Research Council. To understand what the public worries about and how they worry about it is a major step in establishing the effective dialogue that Covello notes is necessary. This panel, composed of people who have spent many years in the arena where this public dialogue is exercised, brings knowledgeable insight to these important issues.

John F. Ahearne, Ph.D., is executive director of Sigma Xi, The Scientific Research Society.

The Need for Effective Communication to Address Public Concerns

• VINCENT T. COVELLO

WITHIN THE LAST FIVE TO 10 YEARS, there have been radical changes in people's concerns about chemicals and what they're doing to our health, our safety, and the environment. Most believe that 80 to 90 percent of all cancers in America are caused by exposures to chemicals in the environment and that less than approximately 10 percent of all cancers are due to life-style factors such as smoking, diet, exercise, and nutrition. Most scientists, however, would argue that 80 to 90 percent of all cancers are due to lifestyle factors and that probably at most 6 to 10 percent can be attributed to exposures to chemicals in the environment. Public concerns also have escalated to problems beyond cancer. We are now talking about not only chemicals causing cancer and a range of different diseases but also chemically induced AIDS. To make matters worse, the government and industry have the lowest level of credibility in the public eye.

Because of this radical change, we are put in a position today of having not only to communicate more often with many more audiences than ever before but also to communicate skillfully. To effectively communicate about these issues, we have to treat communication not as something we do naturally or intuitively well, but as something we do on the basis of our perceiving it as a complex skill.

There are three strategies for effective communication. The first strategy is to win back trust and credibility—a very difficult task once trust has been lost. The second strategy is to draw on the credibility of those who do have credibility in society. The principle is called credibility transference. The last and the most recommended strategy is to enhance your own personal credibility through understanding, practicing, and training in the principles of effective risk communication.

The issue is skill in communication. For example, there are more than 40 traps and pitfalls in effective communication, including ineffective to inappropriate use of risk comparisons. Table 1 provides 10 guidelines for improving the effectiveness of risk comparisons. In addition, there are approximately 77 nonverbal communication skill factors that influence public perceptions of trust and credibility when communicating health, safety, and environmental messages. Another general rule of thumb for effective and skillful communication is to adapt language to the audience. For example, when dealing with the general public, it is useful generally to speak at about the sixth- to ninth-grade level.

Table 1: Guidelines for improving the effectiveness of risk comparisons

1. Target the comparison to a specific audience's needs, concerns, preferences, and level of knowledge.

2. Be specific about the intent of the comparison, and caution against unwarranted conclusions.

3. Explicitly acknowledge and explain relevant assumptions and uncertainties in the calculation of risk estimates.

4. Discuss risk estimates for the worst case, the best case, and the most likely case.

5. Avoid comparisons that ignore factors that influence public perceptions of risk and acceptability, such as voluntariness, fairness, benefits, alternatives, and control.

6. Acknowledge limitations in comparisons that ignore factors that influence public perceptions of risk and acceptability.

7. Focus the comparison on classes of substances, products, processes, or activities that are similar or related in their characteristics, such as activities that serve the same function and whose benefits tend to be similar.

8. Formulate the comparison to illuminate relevant health and environmental consequences, including short-term and long-term effects.

9. Provide information on the socioeconomic consequences of decisions implied by the comparison.

10. Test and evaluate the usefulness of the risk comparison for the target audience.

To communicate effectively we have to treat communication as a skill that requires knowledge, training, and practice.

The lack of sensitivity to communication helps escalate the problem of public concern and hinders the ability to establish dialogue. The whole point of effective communication is to establish an exchange of information—a dialogue—but this is impossible if we are not communicating effectively. To communicate effectively we have to treat communication as a skill, a complex skill that requires knowledge, training, and practice.

Vincent T. Covello, Ph.D., is a professor of environmental sciences in the Center for Risk Communication, School of Public Health and Medicine, Columbia University.

Public and Private Perceptions of Risk

• Michael R. Edelstein

A
S AN "ENVIRONMENTAL PSYCHOLOGIST," I suggest that two ways have evolved for looking at the environment. One perspective looks at the ambient environment, the other the objective environment. The ambient environment is viewed from the perspective of being in it. It surrounds us and we are a part of it. Anything that happens to the environment will also happen to us. By contrast, we view the objective environment as though it were an object out there, separate, distinct, and distant from us. We can measure, manipulate, and exploit it. We can do anything to the objective environment and it has little effect on us.[1]

The tools that we use to look at risk assessment—cost-benefit analysis and other trappings—belong to the objective environmental perspective. As a result, the way that scientists and government officials approach risk—by objectifying the environment in an attempt to control risk—might be construed as part of the environmental problem rather than as offering solutions to it. Furthermore, it is impossible to understand the public's perception of risk from this perspective because risk perception is a reaction to the ambient environment. It cannot be appreciated from a distance and measured objectively. You have to be there.

What we call risk is merely part of the overall fabric of what people experience in the context of their personal lives. To understand an ambient perspective of the environment we need to look at the context of life. People's perception of risk is typically derived from the varied expectations and basic assumptions that underlie their lives. Some people tend to assume that they are healthy until proven otherwise, that they understand and have a lot of personal control over their environment, and that they live in a safe, secure, and just social environment where everyone is treated fairly. The physical environment is an objective entity that can be trusted to be supportive of us when we need it. Over the past decades, however, a new type

60

REGULATING RISK

We need to recognize NIMBY
as a legitimate reaction
to undesirable environmental change.

of human-caused environmental change has occurred on a large scale which disconfirms these basic assumptions.[2]

When we talk about how people perceive risks and why, it is useful to distinguish between the different groups of people we are talking about. There is the "oblivious public," those who still believe in the basic set of expectations listed above. Then there is the "vigilant public," those who particularly look out for risk issues because they fear the consequences of exposure. There are also the "environmental victims," those who think that their normal assumptions have already been destroyed by some type of environmental exposure or contamination and who typically see themselves as victims.

"Environmental victims" commonly convey the impression that outsiders simply do not understand environmental victimization. With victimization, people's daily lives change. They perceive such changes as something that has been done to them, something that has been caused, often by others, something that they have no control over, and something that they fear. Chronic environmental contamination challenges their basic life expectations. Victims now see their health in a very pessimistic frame, redefining past illnesses in terms of the contamination. They reassess the presumption of good health. There is a loss of perceived control over the future. The home comes to be seen as unsafe. The environment is also viewed as dangerous. There is a loss of trust.

Environmental disturbance creates turbulence in people's lives. As a coping effort, people will initially look to others for help who do not have it to give. Not only do social helpers (friends and relatives) prove unable to help victims, but institutional helpers (government and physicians) also fall

Risk assessors and managers need to alter the current "objective" risk management perspective to one of shared risk vigilance.

short. In the end, people who share the same kinds of circumstances pull together and create new organizations and new networks that serve as a basis to regain some of the lost control, offer the support absent from society, and basically provide information and confirmation not available from other sources. NIMBY ("not in my back yard") activities are examples of these coping efforts by victims or the "vigilant public" to avoid becoming environmental victims.

The NIMBY response should be seen in a positive light. In many ways, when professionals talk about risk, what we really want is for people to become vigilant. We want to see them constantly scanning their surroundings, making determinations about what protective actions should be taken. Vigilance is necessary to both individual and societal change in environmental behavior. So we want vigilance. But when we find it in the case of NIMBY, we treat it as a problem, an obstacle. Instead, we need to recognize NIMBY as a legitimate reaction to undesirable environmental change. Instead of "blaming" the vigilant for flagging impacts that government and industry were prepared to ignore, we should confront the substantive issues raised by NIMBY—namely, the quality of the environment after proposed changes would occur.

The NIMBY-bashing reaction illustrates a common misunderstanding of risk. Risk professionals increasingly think about risk from the standpoint of how we understand people in order to control their response. The real challenge of risk assessment, however, is to open up a social dialogue that involves people in ways that avoid the very risk situations that are created by those who manipulate the environment, often with no effective mitigation.

Risk is something that professionals need to think about very differently. Currently, the professionals' "It won't happen" is closest to the oblivious public's "It can't happen to me." Instead, risk assessors and managers need to involve people in the discussion of risk and, in so doing, fundamentally alter the current "objective" risk management perspective to one of shared risk vigilance. This shift would recognize that if there are certain environmental changes that are unacceptable, then perhaps alternative ecological paths need to be found.

---

[1] Thure Von Vexkull, "Ambient and Environment—or Which Is the Correct Perspective on Nature?" (paper presented at the International Association for the Study of People and Their Physical Surroundings, West Berlin, West Germany, July 25-29, 1984).

[2] Michael R. Edelstein, *Contaminated Community: The Social and Psychological Impacts of Residential Toxic Exposure* (Boulder, CO: Westview Press, 1988).

Michael R. Edelstein, Ph.D., is a professor in the School of Social Science and Human Services and is affiliated with the Institute for Environmental Studies, Ramapo College of New Jersey.

The Role of the Media in the Perception of Risk

• CRISTINE RUSSELL

MANY OF THE PROBLEMS WE ENCOUNTER in risk and risk communication depend on the different players in the risk game. What is an expert? We have experts in different institutions, in academia, in industry or funded by industry (sometimes with conflicting findings—the dueling Ph.D.s), and in the government. There are problems with experts and the data they generate in the risk arena, and the conclusion of many studies is that we need more studies (known as the National Academy of Sciences syndrome). We have had problems with confusing statistics in risk; extrapolating animal data to humans; misleading statements about risk, sometimes diverting attention from the real risk; media manipulation; and the choices that the data generate. Translating the expert's language into straight English is another problem. Here is where the media come in.

Virtually every day the general public is presented with a new risk. Old risks stay around and new ones come along, competing for the average person's daily worry budget. To some degree the media are slowly getting more sophisticated in writing or broadcasting risk stories so that there is not a constant risk overload. Increasingly, we have a specialized media covering health, science, and the environment and reporters who have covered so many risk stories that they are getting more skeptical about the sources of information and the degree of risk involved.

This is not to say that a general assignment reporter with little perspective or background or even an experienced reporter with a technical background will not overreact and blow a story out of proportion. The media certainly deserve a certain amount of blame for scaring the public with little perspective on what to worry about and what the priorities are. The stories that make news are often examples of the spectacular, the dramatic, the unknown, and are not necessarily related to their relative public health impor-

Deadlines often leave
little time
to seek the big picture.

tance. Furthermore, deadlines often leave little time to seek the big picture and tend to focus on a single concern. Stories about risk usually involve science on the run. But much of the blame for the haphazard and confusing stories about risk in the media must be shared by the scientists and technical people, their institutions, the politicians, the government bureaucrats, and the competing industry and advocacy groups, all of whom often have axes to grind for a particular purpose.

There is also the problem of the way the public perceives the risk story, and again, we have to keep in mind that there are many publics. Risk for the public is as much a matter of feelings as of facts. The perception of risk is as important as the reality of the risk. A major technological paradox of our time is that it is both the riskiest and the safest of times, as a recent National Academy of Sciences report noted. The paradox emerges from the discrepancy between the experts' and the public's view of risk. While the experts view the world of today as safer than ever before, the public sees life becoming riskier. The dispute cannot be resolved by available evidence. In fact, it may not be about evidence. At a deeper level it is about what kinds of risks people want most to avoid, what kinds of lives they want to lead, what they believe the future will bring, and what the proper relationship is between humanity and nature, according to the report.

In communicating about risk, keep the following issues in mind: How serious is the risk? How many people are potentially affected? Is it a national or a local problem? What is the individual risk? For whom and when might exposure have occurred? How uncertain is the risk? Is it well known or newly discovered? Do the experts agree that there is a risk? How much research needs to be done to get better answers? How long will it take and

A major technological paradox
of our time is that it is both the riskiest
and the safest of times.

what are the consequences of waiting? (Information on public health consequences should be released as quickly, responsibly, and openly as possible.) What is the source of the risk information? What are the risk trade-offs? Who bears the risks and who benefits? Is it voluntary or involuntary? What hat is the expert wearing? (We need to distinguish scientific findings from personal judgments, to distinguish risk assessment from risk management issues when possible.) What is society doing about the risk? What is the cost of reducing or eliminating it? What about industry? What can the individual do about it?

These are all questions that ought to be asked more often. I would like to hope that people would have the answers.

Cristine Russell is a special health correspondent to the Washington Post.

PART 6

Responding to Risk: How Politics, Economics, and Perceptions Affect Public Policy

INTRODUCTION BY JOHN D. GRAHAM

I n this session we are going to examine some difficult questions: What do we do about risk? How do we respond to risks? And what role do economics and politics play in shaping the strategies we exercise in responding to risk?

The panelists represent a rich blend of expertise and real-world experience as researchers, policy makers, and risk managers. Each has been asked to present his or her perspective on the shaping of risk policy. In addition, each presenter has been challenged to address these questions: Does it all make sense? Are public policies on risk doing things in a sensible way?

The panel has been organized to include two scholars, if you will, on the subject of risk management. The panel also includes two practitioners actively involved in the politics of risk management.

Lester Lave, a professor of economics at Carnegie-Mellon University, examines the issue of misplaced priorities. Why are policies focusing on relatively trivial risks while ignoring major risks?

Paul Slovic is the president of Decision Research, and his research focuses on factors that shape the public perception of risk. His presentation emphasizes the importance of public values and trust in the development of risk management policies.

Molly Coye, as director of the California Department of Health Services, faces daily decision making regarding public risks. Her presentation reminds us that many risk decisions have been shaped by the narrow focus of quantitative risk assessment and underscores the need for a sound public health basis for risk decision making.

William Schultz is counsel to the Subcommittee on Health and Environment of the U.S. House of Representatives. His presentation provides an inside look at the risk policy-making process and examines the factors that determine the political agenda for risk management.

John D. Graham, Ph.D., is Professor of Policy and Decision Sciences in the Center for Risk Analysis, Harvard School of Public Health.

Integrating the Public in Public Health Decision Making

• MOLLY JOEL COYE

HERE ARE MANY REASONS to integrate public health concerns into risk management. The environment is a public health issue, as well as an issue involving land use and economic development, the protection of other species, physical recreation, and many other factors. Yet these non-health-related concerns have dominated environmental decisions over the past few decades, whereas public health concerns have largely been ignored.

In its broadest sense, public health is the interface between science and politics. Public health officials make decisions concerning alternative uses of public resources to promote and improve the health of the public. In each situation where the environment is potentially hazardous, public health agencies must determine the extent of exposure, public knowledge and levels of concern, the potential for harm involved, the urgency with which problems must be addressed, and alternative means of protection with regard to the feasibility and the cost of protecting the public from a potential harm. This public health evaluation should be a key component of the initial site evaluation, and lay the groundwork for establishment of priorities for site studies and remediation, for immediate action, and for longer-term planning.

We cannot escape the fact that this is a public process as well as a scientific process. All public policies should be able to withstand scrutiny of their rationale and their results. In the case of hazardous waste sites, removing or mitigating potential harm to the health of the public has been a principal rationale for the creation of public programs and for requirements imposed on private entities. Yet neither the process of site evaluation nor the results of site remediation meet the test of protecting the public's health. Under the existing Superfund policy, the public health assessment is not conducted un-

The environment
is a public issue.

til several years after sites are initially identified, and then only if the site has been proposed for the Superfund list. Of the 500,000 known sites, only 33,000 sites are on the CERCLA (Comprehensive Environmental Response, Compensation and Liability Act) list and only 1500 sites have been identified on the Superfund list. Therefore, most of the sites have never received a public health assessment.

Our narrow focus on risk assessment and risk management has allowed us to obfuscate issues. We have not employed the traditional elements of sound public health strategy—that is, the discovery and preliminary assessment of as many sites as possible, the description and prioritization of the universe of potential exposures and harm, the development of remediation programs, and continuous attention to risk communication. Instead, we regard the numbers produced by traditional Superfund risk assessment as all we need to know about the characterization of sites, and we never go beyond risk management to deal with the very substantial issues of risk communication.

Despite the substantial amounts of money spent on remediation, we have not applied the most important sciences of public health—epidemiology and toxicology—to these decisions. In addition to the information currently used for risk assessments, we need data from surrounding-area exposure assessments, as well as clinical assessments incorporating approaches from occupational medicine and toxicology. These data constitute the scientific basis necessary for individual site decisions and for building the foundations of sound policies.

Furthermore, the concerns and questions of policy makers—legislators, agency directors, and the courts—must be addressed in the development and conduct of site evaluation processes. Their questions are not limited to risk assessment numbers, but require estimates of potential human harm, community concern, and the political and economic implications of the options before them. Policy makers would like our best information on how widespread the problem may be, how serious the threat to human health may be, which sites may present the worst problems and should be dealt with first, and what the concerns of the community are—in short, what is the most that can be accomplished with limited resources to protect public health.

Our treatment of the recently discovered chromium contamination of landfills in New Jersey is a good example of a public health approach to an environmental problem. There are about 4 billion pounds of chromium in the urban environment in that state, and the cleanup cost estimate runs well into the billions. The risk assessment number itself—the level of contamination in the soil—played only a small role in our decision on how much to spend on remediation. Occupational medicine experience, toxicology, and direct work with the community played a much more important role. Medical consultations and evaluations, careful exposure measurements, long-term commitment to follow-up with the community, and targeted occupational health studies were essential components of a sound public health approach.

Ultimately, community surveillance and community involvement in this entire process—including decisions on remediation—will determine the success of our efforts. Without community involvement, it is very likely that in New Jersey we would have found ourselves in a confrontational situation requiring large expenditures on untargeted, politically driven cleanups. With a public health approach, we were able to truly assess the potential risk to the population, and to let that information drive our public policies.

Molly Joel Coye, M.D., M.P.H., is director of the California Department of Health Services.

Fixing the System

• LESTER B. LAVE

AMERICA'S RISK MANAGEMENT SYSTEM is broken. Risk management in the United States has developed as individual responses, public and private, to individual situations. Little or no thought has been given to focusing on the worst problems or on lowering risks efficiently. Rather, the system has been driven by public horror at traumatic injuries and chronic disease. We reach out to those in need.

The result is a hodgepodge of individual decisions. There is no consistency across decisions. Attention is focused on minor risks while some major risks are ignored. Our scholars and public and private leaders have not translated the public's concern into sensible programs to manage risks better.

Public Concerns Versus Expert Analysis. The public is concerned with toxic waste dumps, carcinogenic chemicals in air, water, and food, and nuclear power plants. In recent years, we have had social spasms concerning Alar, dioxin, and ethylene dibromide; in retrospect, all of these risks were overstated and the concern might have done more harm than good.

Health experts agree that carcinogenic chemicals in the environment cause perhaps 1-2 percent of cancers in the United States and that there is little public harm from toxic waste dumps. Nuclear power plants are among the safest current technologies for generating electricity.

While lavishing concern on these low-risk situations, people have turned away from highway crashes and tobacco use. The former kill more than 40,000 people each year, and the latter is the largest cause of premature death in the United States. Highway crashes are the leading killer of children and young adults. Tobacco use results in more than a third of the 1 million new cancers in the United States each year.

Most people have done little to modify their diet to lower both their cancer and cardiovascular disease risks. Dietary change would prevent more than 330,000 cancers each year. We give almost no attention to indoor air pollutants, including radon.

The media and some well-meaning
but uncritical scientists
have fanned the fires of public concern.

Scientists have developed a solid foundation for developing programs to prevent this sea of cancers and traumatic deaths. In many cases, the costs are zero or are modest. Certainly there are some life-style changes that would be needed, such as buckling seat belts and eating food with less fat. We know that these life-style changes are possible, since about 50 percent of people now buckle their seat belts, about five times as many as 10 years ago. We know that many people have given up smoking and have changed to a healthier diet.

Governmental and private risk managers agree with these facts, but many protest that this picture is too simplistic. The public is worried about toxic waste dumps and not worried about highway crashes and indoor air pollution. Agency heads conclude that we must do as the public wishes, even if this is contrary to the experts' judgment.

Certainly a democracy must attend to citizen concerns. But we also have to consider the source of those concerns and the information they are based on. The media and some well-meaning but uncritical scientists have fanned the fires of public concern about "unseen killers unleashed by malevolent corporations." The Environmental Protection Agency has estimated that its regulations on toxic chemicals might prevent up to 6500 cancers per year. Thus, EPA might conceivably prevent fewer than 1 percent of cancers in the United States by its regulations.

At the same time, government regulation has increased expenditures to clean up Superfund sites to almost $10 billion per year. The 1990 Clean Air Act is estimated to impose costs of more than $20 billion per year to reduce emissions of "hazardous air pollutants." These large expenditures will prevent cancers and other diseases measured in the hundreds, not the hundreds of thousands.

EPA recognized this problem in 1986 and undertook a study to set agency priorities. That study was redone in 1990 and EPA Administrator Reilly sought congressional approval to shift funds away from areas where expenditures result in little improvement in health or environmental quality. Everyone agrees that more resources must go to educating the public about health and environmental risks so that more intelligent government decisions and private decisions can be made.

Highway Risks. The management of highway risks is slightly better than the management of toxic chemicals in the environment. Since 1985, nearly every state has implemented a requirement that front-seat occupants buckle their seat belts. In New York, belt use is at about 70 percent, but it is considerably lower in some other states. A series of studies have demonstrated that mandatory belt use laws save lives. They show that states that have "strong" belt use laws have higher belt use and fewer highway deaths. We know how to prevent many highway deaths.

Even when people are wearing a three-point seat belt, air bags can increase safety. In fact, adding an air bag to a car where the occupants are belted will save lives at a cost of less than $1 million per premature death. This sum is small compared with the social expenditures of saving lives in many other situations.

Almost half of all fatal highway crashes involve a driver who is drunk. Many of these crashes could be prevented by improving enforcement of the current laws against driving while intoxicated.

Finally, most crashes are ascribed to driver error. This notion is misleading. If automobiles and highways were designed for Grand Prix drivers, virtually all crashes would be due to driver error. If, however, automobiles and highways were designed for 70-year-old drivers with poor eyesight and slow reaction times, almost no crashes would be due to driver error. The current system can be unforgiving if a driver is attending to the car stereo or is otherwise momentarily distracted. Many crashes could be prevented by improving signs and otherwise making the system more forgiving.

Conclusion. The risk management system is broken. None of these observations or examples is new. The relevant government agencies and corporations know about the misallocation of resources in their area and the steps that can be taken to manage risks better. Our risk management system is broken because little has been done or is being done to fix these problems.

To repair the current system, society must begin with priorities about which areas are important. To a first approximation, each premature death is equally important to prevent. As we look into priority setting, we will discover that some premature deaths are more important than others. We would prefer to prevent the death of a 25-year-old woman with young children compared with a 75-year-old. We seem to value preventing cancer deaths more than highway deaths.

To set these priorities, a great deal of effort is needed to understand what the public is concerned about and what is the basis for this concern. People cannot set priorities unless they are reasonably informed about risks of common technologies, industrial facilities, consumer goods, foods, and actions. Educating people about these risks is complicated because a complicated array of decisions is needed. Although it is not possible to make every American into a risk expert, much could be done to inform people so that they could make better decisions—decisions that they believe reflect their values.

In parallel with the effort to educate the public, government agencies and corporations must take a more systematic approach to risk management. The premature deaths, injuries, and disease that can be prevented at relatively low cost should receive attention and resources. More generally, Americans must decide that managing risks is too important to be left to emotional reactions. Our health and limbs are too important to be left to an uninformed, unsystematic process of risk management.

Lester B. Lave, Ph.D., is James H. Higgins Professor of Economics and University Professor in the Graduate School of Industrial Administration, Carnegie-Mellon University.

Public Perception
and the Legislative Process

• WILLIAM B. SCHULTZ

I T IS USEFUL TO BEGIN with the familiar statistic that one-third of the cancers diagnosed annually in the United States are related to diet, one-third are caused by tobacco, and one-third are caused by environmental exposures. Companies that use carcinogenic chemicals argue that their contribution is small compared with the contribution of tobacco and food. In other words, their strategy is to shift the "blame" from industry to consumers.

This is an old and familiar argument. For example, before Ralph Nader wrote his book *Unsafe at Any Speed*, which demonstrated that car accidents are caused by defective automobile design, the automobile industry had successfully persuaded the public that car accidents were caused by driver error. Nader's work shifted our thinking about automobile safety, providing the impetus for enactment of the National Motor Vehicle Safety Act. That law pushed much of the responsibility for automobile injuries on the car companies, and as a result automobiles are much safer today than they were 25 years ago.

We have the opportunity to make the same kind of progress with respect to industrial exposures to cancer-causing chemicals. Take Alar as an example. In 1987, the National Academy of Sciences reviewed the risks of pesticides and identified 27 with a particularly high risk. The report indicated that Alar's risk was greater than the 27 pesticides combined.

Several factors account for the public outcry about Alar. First of all, many children consume huge amounts of apple juice. Second, the risk from Alar came as a big surprise, Third, people were particularly angry when they found out that the EPA had had these data for more than five years. Last, Alar has no significant benefits; there is no evidence that apple yields have gone down since Alar was banned.

It is a sad commentary on government regulation that the chemical and agriculture industries stopped using Alar before the EPA got around to banning it. Although Alar is often used as an example of public overreaction to a relatively small hazard, I believe that the public was reacting in large part to the revelation that the government was not protecting them. Realizing that they could not rely on EPA, people took matters into their own hands and stopped eating apples. The Alar experience demonstrates how all sides can benefit from amendments to our pesticide laws that require EPA to act quickly against potentially dangerous pesticides. Consumers will get more protection, and the public's confidence in the process will protect industry against future Alar-like scares.

I am often asked what factors determine which issues get addressed by Congress. There are six that I have identified. The first one is the merits. Every issue that comes up is argued first on the merits. The second factor is the political muscle of the interest groups involved. The third factor is consumer muscle. The fourth is that it is a lot easier to block new legislation than to change an existing law. The fifth is the interest of the chairman or chairwoman of the relevant committee. They set the agenda, they call the hearings, and they have a very big impact on what gets through. Finally, the skill of the legislators working on the issue is critical. Often there are real opportunities for compromise that a skilled legislator can identify and exploit.

William B. Schultz is counsel for the Subcommittee on Health and the Environment, Committee on Energy and Commerce, U.S. House of Representatives. The views in this summary are Mr. Schultz's and do not necessarily reflect the views of any member of the subcommittee.

Risk Assessment and the Public Trust

• PAUL SLOVIC

P ERCEPTIONS CERTAINLY DO INFLUENCE POLICY. The Environmental Protection Agency has come out with several studies saying that it is more influenced by the perceptions of the public than by its own assessments of what really should be the priority hazards on its agenda.

Perceptions should influence policy not just because occasionally experts are wrong and the public is right, but also because perceptions reflect legitimate values. Qualities such as whether or not a risk is voluntary and controllable, issues of equity, catastrophic potential, and the known-versus-unknown factor—all are important in the public's responses to risk.

Perceptions have impacts, and risk assessment needs to consider them. With regard to impact, individual risk perceptions and cognitions sometimes interact with social and institutional forces to trigger massive social and economic impacts in response to events; even small incidents can have major impacts.

Perceptions feed the social amplification of risk. The implication of this is that policies must yield protection above and beyond what might be judged worthwhile by traditional risk analysis. For example, social amplification drives policy toward prevention rather than just containment of accidents. Amplification gives advantage to remote siting, dedicated trains, and tamper-resistant packaging policies.

Another reason for paying attention to perceptions is that policies that ignore perceptions may prove to be ineffective. For instance, the federal nuclear waste policy is facing serious difficulties because it has continually ignored public perceptions, relying almost exclusively on technical assessments of risk. Politicians who ignore public perceptions do so at their peril.

Last, but not least, is the important issue of trust. The acceptance of any risk is more dependent on public confidence in risk management than on quantitative estimates of risk. The most significant quality of trust is its fragility. It is far easier to destroy trust than to create it; sources of bad news are typically more credible than sources of good news; and it is easier to demonstrate risk than safety. Furthermore, our society systematically obliterates trust in risk management. For example, media reporting of problems worldwide in nuclear, chemical, and other areas destroys trust. So does our adversarial risk management, which is based on litigation that pits expert against expert who knock down each other's models and theories. So do the special interest groups that bring problems to the spotlight and keep them there. We have a great political system in many ways, but in the risk area, where safety is so hard to demonstrate, the system tends to damage trust. I am not saying that our system is necessarily a bad one—merely that loss of trust is one of its consequences.

In order to really make progress in risk management, we have to confront the problem of trust directly and give it top priority. We must recognize that loss of trust is not due to ignorance or irrationality, that public relations will not produce trust, and that risk communication will not work without it.

Trust is in a sense more fundamental than risk communication. If you have trust, you do not need elaborate communication. If you do not have trust, any form of message is unlikely to be successful.

To date we have not adequately appreciated the importance of trust. We must recognize that to get anywhere in risk policy, we have to have the willing consent of a public that has control and is part of the decision-making process. Until Congress, federal agencies, and industries recognize the reality of perception and trust, our experiences with risk management will continue to be contentious and unsatisfying.

Paul Slovic, Ph.D., is president of Decision Research, in Eugene, Oregon, and is professor of psychology at the University of Oregon.

PART 7

Managing Risks in the Future: Where Do We Go from Here?

INTRODUCTION BY THOMAS P. GRUMBLY

W hat do we do about the present crisis of public perception concerning hazardous waste sites and the lack of public trust in government and industry? What is the public's bottom-line "acceptable risk," and where is there a specific risk number that people are willing to accept? What is the role of numbers in the risk game, and how important should they be? Have we arrived at the state of "analysis paralysis" so that all of what we are doing with risk assessment and risk comparison is to shield us from taking necessary actions? How can we be innovative and move forward to improve the public health and welfare? These are some of the very difficult questions that we are confronted with today. Our ability to manage risks in the future will depend on how well we address these issues.

In this section four individuals representing different perspectives on managing risks tackle this very important question: "Where do we go from here?" Representing industry's perspectives are Larry Boggs and Jim Emerson. Larry Boggs has been an attorney for General Electric since 1988. Before that, he was with the American Mining Congress. Jim Emerson is the director of External Technical Affairs for The Coca-Cola Company. For a labor group's perspective, we have Frank Mirer, director of Health and Safety for the United Auto Workers Union, who has a unique perspective on both the scientific and the practical aspects of trying to deal with risk in an economic world. For independent views we can look to Paul Portney of Resources for the Future, an economic and natural resources analysis organization in Washington D.C.

Joan Claybrook, president of the public interest group Public Citizen, and Michael Taylor, an attorney with the law firm King and Spalding at the time of the conference and now deputy commissioner for policy at the U.S. Food and Drug Administration, also made presentations at this session but were unable to complete the edited versions of their remarks.

Thomas P. Grumbly, Ph.D., is president of Clean Sites, Inc.

Weighing the Costs and the Benefits

• PAUL R. PORTNEY

A CCORDING TO THE ENVIRONMENTAL PROTECTION AGENCY, the annual compliance cost for federal environmental regulations was about 2.1 percent of the gross national product in 1990. This is expected to increase to approximately 2.8 percent of the GNP in the year 2000. Just because that is a big number, however, does not mean that we are overregulating across the board. There are environmental regulations that easily justify themselves. There are, however, those that require so much sacrifice to put in place that we cannot come close to justifying them.

For future success in risk management, we must find ways to weigh benefits and costs to strike the appropriate balance in how far to pursue risk regulations. The existing environmental and other risk-regulating statutes do not provide a convenient mechanism for doing this. Most statutes explicitly prohibit the balancing of benefits and costs in setting standards. This is also one cause for the tension between the executive branch and Congress over risk regulations.

Although I am not suggesting that we express everything quantitatively in dollars and cents to balance benefits and costs, we should change our statutes to allow regulatory decision makers to make qualitatively balanced judgments. This is the basis for sensible government regulation.

Paul R. Portney, Ph.D., is vice-president of Resources for the Future.

Reexamining Risk Assessment Decisions

• LARRY A. BOGGS

FOR NONTHRESHOLD POLLUTANTS there is no alternative to risk assessment as a decision tool in the legislative and regulatory context. Therefore, we need to have a reliable and acceptable means of assessing risk, and this is primarily a scientific function.

Risk assessment is not a static process. Although regulatory agencies cannot constantly reevaluate risk assessment issues, there has to be a means by which they can periodically reexamine risk assessments for particular substances and the regulatory decisions that grow out of them in light of new evidence and information. Because regulatory decisions are based on the best available information at the time of the decisions, we should have the right to revisit the issue as new information becomes available.

Although risk assessment is an extremely important step in the process of risk management, the real policy decisions are ultimately made by society. We are operating on the edge of science where there is an incredible amount of uncertainty. Furthermore, we operate in a world economy where there are important economic consequences that result from our risk management policy decisions.

Larry A. Boggs is counsel for Environmental Legislative and Regulatory Affairs, Corporate Environmental Programs, General Electric Company.

Refining the Scientific Basis for Risk Assessment

• JAMES L. EMERSON

A S WE LOOK AT RISK ASSESSMENT in the day-to-day world, we frequently find that there is a lack of biological data integrated into the risk assessment process. Risk assessment is no better than the science that goes into it. Industry, government, and other parties involved have a responsibility to develop and use a risk assessment process that is based on sound, credible science, as opposed to theoretical assumptions and models. We must appreciate that science is an evolving process, which means that the risk assessment number also has to change as new scientific information becomes available. Frequently, we want more from science than what science can actually deliver. Therein lies the potential for conflict of opinion and interpretation. It is the responsibility of all of us to effectively communicate risks.

Risks have to be prioritized so that limited resources can be most effectively utilized to resolve some of the problems that we face as a nation, especially in the public health arena. We can spend an inordinate amount of money over a period of five or 10 years on a specific issue. We should carefully evaluate the process and ask the basic questions: What has been accomplished by our action or by the risk assessment process? Have the resources been spent wisely—and are the results what we anticipated? We need to examine the entire process and its impact with more rigor than we have in the past. This process can be extremely expensive, and we are going to have to become much more selective in a time of diminishing resources.

James L. Emerson, D.V.M., Ph.D., is director of External Technical Affairs, The Coca-Cola Company.

Is Risk Assessment Diluting Public Health Protection?

• FRANKLIN E. MIRER

T HE CURRENT FLURRY OF DISCUSSIONS about risk assessment and the reordering of priorities for environmental protection is part of a counterattack against public health protection. The decades-old complaint of overregulation is currently backed by false claims that new science proves that risks of hazards from chemical exposure are generally overestimated. The new attacks are a part of a long-term plan to encumber the process of public health regulation with such complex and difficult steps before action can be taken that nothing happens.

Risk assessment differs depending on whether it is applied to an Occupational Safety and Health Administration standard, environmental regulations, a Superfund site, a drug approval, a vehicle safety standard, or liability insurance, yet the same term is used. The broad offensive against public health regulation to prevent chemical exposure is advanced under the banner of revising approaches to risk assessment. The offensive uses a twofold strategy: 1) repackage all of the old arguments against the use of animal studies under claims of new science to discredit the entire process of carcinogen risk assessment, and 2) construct ad hoc arguments based on unproven hypotheses regarding mechanisms of action to explain away the risks of particular chemicals, such as formaldehyde, gasoline, and methylene chloride. The latter approach is now attractive to the Environmental Protection Agency.

The major point is that there is not any substantial new body of science that calls into question the past general approach to risk assessment for carcinogens. However, more chemicals have been shown to be carcinogenic through animal tests. There are many new studies of people, especially workers, showing increased cancer likely due to chemical exposure. The new science, in fact, indicates that we should be doing more, not less.

The relationship between risk assessment and management is distorted.

Risk assessment and risk management must be iterative processes and not disconnected. Instead, risk assessment has become a hurdle that must be jumped before risk management options can be considered. As a result, readily solvable chemical exposure problems remain because risk management options are not considered early enough in the process.

Franklin E. Mirer, Ph.D., is the director of the Health and Safety Department, United Auto Workers Union.

PART 8

Regulating Risk:
The Challenges Ahead

• THOMAS A. BURKE

The conference on "Regulating Risk: The Science and Politics of Risk" represented an unprecedented opportunity for the nation's thought leaders in risk policy to probe the scientific and social underpinnings of the decision-making process. Participants represented the perspectives of the public, government, business, the media, public interest groups, and the scientific community. The conference brought together experts in public health, safety, and risk assessment to provide a unique view of the contrast between traditional approaches to health and safety and current approaches to quantitative risk assessment.

The uneasy marriage of science and policy that is so characteristic of the risk management process provided the backdrop for the conference. The discussions were punctuated by spirited exchanges and more than a few disagreements. Not surprisingly, the views of presenters were diverse and underlined the complexity of the social, economic, and scientific barriers to successful risk management. Yet despite the diversity of backgrounds and disagreements over approaches, the participants presented a number of constructive recommendations for the development of more effective ways to measure, characterize, and communicate risks.

THE GOAL OF REGULATING RISK

The traditional goal of regulating risks is to protect and improve public health and welfare. As the number of measurable and perceived risks continues to spiral, however, a more expansive and elusive goal has emerged. Effective risk regulation must be responsive to public values, include a commitment to communication, and integrate scientific, social, and economic concerns while still protecting public health. Unfortunately, current approaches to risk management have fallen short of this goal.

In his presentation, Lester Lave bluntly stated that the risk management system in this country is "broken." While most speakers were not quite as harsh in their criticism, the consensus was clear: the current risk regulation process needs change.

Risk management is defined in the National Academy of Sciences report *Risk Assessment in the Federal Government* as "the process of evaluating alternative regulatory options and selecting among them."[1] Risk regulation is a multistep process that ideally includes risk assessment, risk management, and risk communication. The process is neither unidirectional nor free from social values and perceptions, economic considerations, communications and miscommunications, and political influences. At virtually every step, the process is easy to criticize but difficult to improve.

Predictably, the conference produced many points of view on the current state of risk regulation. Table 1 contains a sampling of the many recommendations for refining the process presented by speakers throughout the conference.

THE THEMES FOR CHANGE

The wide range of recommendations reflects the complexity of risk regulation. The recommendations, quite predictably, tend to reflect the expertise or interests of the presenters. The scientists called for strengthening the risk assessment component, the economists and the regulated community stressed the need for improved measures of cost effectiveness, and communication experts warned that failure to improve communication and trust can undermine the credibility of the entire process.

Despite the diversity of opinions and approaches, a number of common threads are evident throughout the presentations. Four themes emerge from the presentations that seemed to provide a framework for the discussions, criticisms, and recommendations for change (see Table 2). The following sections present a brief overview of these themes

---

Table 1. Recommendations to improve risk regulation

- Define the role of science in the regulatory process.
- Reduce the uncertainty of current risk estimates.
- Improve current estimates of human exposures.
- Refine the risk characterization process.
- Expand the information presented to decision makers.
- Present the full range of risk estimates.
- Improve the cost effectiveness of risk regulation.
- Balance the benefits with the costs of regulation.
- Allocate resources to major public health issues.
- Expand comparative risk approach to priority setting.
- Strengthen the public health basis for decisions.
- Emphasize primary prevention.
- Recognize and respond to public outrage.
- Involve the public throughout the process.
- Develop public trust in risk management.
- Develop more effective approaches to risk communication.
- Define "acceptable" risk.
- Develop more consistent approaches to risk assessment.
- Coordinate agency risk policies.

STRENGTHENING THE SCIENCE

It has often been stated that science should be the driving force behind risk decisions. Although this may be a desirable goal, in fact the current state of risk assessment science is in turmoil. Fundamental questions have been raised about many of the assumptions that have been the basis for federal risk assessment practices. Issues such as thresholds for carcinogens, the use

Table 2. Themes for change

1. Strengthening the science
2. Recognizing and incorporating public values
3. Balancing costs
4. Harmonizing policies

and interpretation of animal data, and the validity of exposure assessments have fueled a spirited debate within the scientific community.

The lack of agreement on risks has frustrated policy makers and contributed to the erosion of public trust in risk management strategies. Congress is currently debating legislation to improve the coordination and scientific oversight of federal risk assessment practices. At the same time, committees have been convened at the National Academy of Sciences and the Office of Technology Assessment to evaluate risk assessment methods and research.

Recognition of the limitations of risk assessment is key to the successful application of science in public policy. The present state of the art does not offer the "bright lines" that decision makers seek when faced with questions about the acceptability of risks. Perhaps one of the most difficult questions in regulating risks is "Where does the science end and the politics begin?" This is by no means a new question. Almost a decade has passed since the NAS "Red Book" made this recommendation: "Regulatory agencies should take steps to establish and maintain a clear conceptual distinction between assessment of risks and the consideration of risk management alternatives; that is, the scientific findings and policy judgments embodied in the risk assessments should be explicitly distinguished from the political, economic, and technical considerations that influence the design and choice of regulatory strategies."

Bernard Goldstein discussed the role of science in risk regulation. He observed that the conference was not a scientific meeting, but rather a risk management meeting dealing with communication and politics. He questioned the role of science in the current reactionary regulatory climate and

Recognition of the limitations of risk assessment is key to the successful application of science in public policy.

cited the technology-based approach of the Clean Air Act as an example of the exclusion of scientific information in risk regulation. He called for a refocusing of current thinking on the scientific base of risk assessment, and stressed that science is most useful in advancing the process when the emphasis is on primary prevention.

Roger McClellan seconded the preventive approach, calling for a future-oriented approach for risk assessment aimed at understanding biologic mechanisms and identifying potential risks from new products, drugs, or environmental exposures.

Joseph Rodricks pointed out that much of the scientific information available on risks currently plays no role in regulatory decision making because it is often not presented to decision makers. The current emphasis on upper-bound risk estimates has limited the data used to calculate risks. He called for a more complete presentation of all available data, including a full range of potential risk estimates and a description of the strengths and weaknesses of the scientific database. Such an approach would allow policy makers a fuller understanding of the scientific issues and limitations and could ultimately lead to improved decision making.

There was little disagreement that the improvement of risk science to reduce uncertainty will benefit the regulatory process. However, frustration with the risk assessment process was apparent. Several speakers urged a return to the basic public health principles of prevention and concentration of efforts on the well-recognized risks facing society. Cristine Russell cautioned against the "National Academy of Sciences syndrome" where each study generates a need for more studies. Ralph Nader called risk assessment a movement toward "massive overcomplication and overabstraction" that attempts to make precise something that by nature cannot be precise.

Despite the differences of opinion, continued efforts to reduce the scientific uncertainty of risk estimates are essential to improving decision making. Ultimately, the credibility and public health effectiveness of the process depends on a strong scientific basis. Recommendations that were presented for strengthening the role of science in risk regulation include refinement of exposure measurements, improved measurement of public health impacts on both individuals and populations, improved translation of the science for the public, and more complete presentation of all available scientific information to decision makers.

COMMUNICATION AND INCORPORATION OF PUBLIC VALUES

Increasing the consideration of public values, encouraging public participation, dealing with outrage, and developing trust are among the most difficult challenges to effective risk management. At the root of these challenges is the need to develop more effective two-way communication between the scientific community, decision makers, and the public.

Peter Sandman pointed out that what risk assessors mean by risk is not necessarily what everyone else means by risk. Public attitudes are shaped by the degree of outrage associated with a risk. He added that the public demands that high-outrage risks be taken more seriously than low-outrage risks, regardless of the opinions of risk assessors. The use of risk assessment to downplay public concerns about risk may only serve to increase outrage. Therefore, risk regulation, to be effective, must develop better ways to manage both outrage and hazard.

Cristine Russell also pointed out the gap between the experts' views and the public's views of risk. The gap has been fueled by continual disagreement among experts and by media stories that have emphasized the spectacular, dramatic, and the unknown but that have not necessarily presented the relative public health importance of risks.

Vincent Covello presented video examples of news coverage of risk, and called for communication to be more than an afterthought of the regulatory process. He called for the recognition of risk communication as a

Communication should be more than an afterthought of the regulatory process.

complex skill that requires knowledge, training, and practice.

Paul Slovic explained that the risk perception gap is a more fundamental issue than is risk communication. He pointed out that if you have trust you do not need elaborate communication. Conversely, without trust any form of message is unlikely to be successful.

Should public perceptions influence risk policies? The answer is that such influence is unavoidable in a democratic society. Risk regulators, however, have a long way to go to improve communication and gain public confidence. From the presentations at the conference, it is clear that the issue of trust has not yet been confronted by government or industry. Future regulatory approaches to risk must recognize the importance of public values, and must accept the public as a partner in the decision-making process.

BALANCING COSTS

Virtually all human activities involve some degree of risk. Decisions regarding which risks to regulate and what costs of regulation are acceptable are among the most difficult issues facing decision makers. Traditionally, risk regulation has not included a thorough analysis of costs and benefits. As the costs of compliance with risk regulations have spiraled, there is an increasing need to balance the costs and benefits of regulating risks.

Although it is convenient and sometimes dramatic to point to the enormous costs of regulatory compliance, the articulation of the benefits remains a challenge. The benefits of regulation, such as improved quality of life and a cleaner environment, are often difficult to quantify and are laden with public values. This has led to a wide diversity of opinion on how costs should be considered in the regulatory process.

How much can society afford to spend to reduce risks? What is an acceptable cost per life saved? How should costs be factored into the priority-setting process? These are just a few of the controversial questions discussed at the conference. The speakers provided an excellent overview of current thinking and a sampling of the divergence of opinion on the issues surrounding the costs of regulation.

Richard Belzer, of the Office of Management and Budget, said that regulatory policies should focus on cost-effective regulations that offer more risk reduction benefits than costs to society. He explained that the primary reason OMB is concerned about risk assessment and risk management is that the "coercive powers of the federal government are being misallocated." The cost effectiveness of federal regulatory proposals, he said, can range from $100,000 to $5.7 trillion per premature death averted. He challenged the conference participants with this fundamental question: "Are the gains from reducing risks really worth these enormous expenditures of scarce societal resources?"

Paul Portney stated that future success in risk management will depend on the development of ways to weigh benefits and costs and to strike the appropriate balance in defining how far to pursue risk regulations. He pointed out the major impediment to such an approach: most statutes explicitly prohibit the agencies from balancing benefits and costs in setting standards. He cautioned against a purely quantitative approach to balancing costs and benefits and recommended that statutes be changed to allow regulatory decision makers to make sensible qualitative balancing judgments.

Frederick Allen talked about the difficult process of setting risk priorities, and presented the Environmental Protection Agency's comparative risk approach as a tool to guide the targeting of resources. A fundamental principle of this approach is that EPA should target its regulatory efforts toward those problems that pose the greatest risks to health and the environment. This approach has been heralded as a means to redefine national priorities toward more cost-effective control of risks.

Allen described the two key questions in comparative risk: What are the most important risks, and what do the people want? He explained that the ultimate success of the comparative risk approach will depend on the an-

Most statutes explicitly prohibit the agencies from balancing benefits and costs in setting standards.

swers to these questions and on the ability of decision makers to strike a balance between public values and the technical assessment of risk.

There appeared to be consensus that resources should be directed toward problems that pose the greatest risks to public health and the environment. However, strong sentiments against the cost-benefit approach to achieve efficiency and set priorities in risk management were expressed by several speakers. Ellen Silbergeld called for the removal of economics from center stage in the risk debate. She stated that it is time to return economics to its proper function as a tool to accomplish goals, rather than using it as a driving force that attempts to define what those goals should be. She and other speakers including Molly Coye called for greater involvement of the public health community and a return to traditional public health principles to guide decision making.

Ralph Nader pointed out the difficulty in defining "cost" and criticized conventional estimates of the costs of regulation as arbitrary. He also warned against the "overmonetization of our social conscience and our social policies."

No approach to risk management can ignore the need to consider the impact of cost on the ultimate success or failure of regulation. The question, however, remains, "To what extent should cost drive risk management priorities?" Without more accurate measurements of the public health and environmental benefits, the spiraling costs of regulation may continue to dominate the debate and shape the national agenda for risk management.

HARMONIZATION OF POLICIES

Different agencies approach the assessment and regulation of risk in different ways. This is not only true at the federal level: the diversity is perhaps most obvious at the state level. Many of the differences are directly due to the specific legislative mandates that define how agencies should approach risk. It must be recognized that the regulation of risks has many facets that may defy a consistent definition of "acceptable risk." For example, the task of safeguarding the food supply is fundamentally different from the task of establishing hazardous waste cleanup standards or regulating the workplace. Although all three approaches may draw on a common scientific database, the decision-making process is ultimately guided by different information on level of risk, legal requirements, feasibility, and cost.

Another aspect of risk regulation that is highly variable and difficult to define is the "philosophy" of risk management. For example, the primary mission of a public health agency is the reduction and prevention of health risks. Therefore risk decisions at such an agency may be guided by a "philosophy" of prevention that may not necessarily consider cost or technical feasibility. Although the prevention of risks may also be a goal of agencies such as the departments of Energy and Transportation or the OMB, the risk management "philosophy" of those departments is necessarily influenced by their primary mission.

There are many aspects of risk regulation that have led to inconsistencies in risk management. Fred Shank provided an excellent example when he contrasted the approaches to aflatoxin and saccharin under the Delaney Amendment. Driven by the mandate of the Delaney Amendment, the Food and Drug Administration proposed to ban saccharin while naturally occurring aflatoxin, which is many orders of magnitude more carcinogenic, was not subject to the same zero tolerance approach.

Henry Habicht spoke of the lack of coherence in environmental policies that constrains the efforts of EPA to put risks into a context that can be compared and contrasted for priority setting. While acknowledging the difficulties of harmonization given the existing laws, he called for more consistency in the risk assessment process and consensus building among risk scientists.

D. Allan Bromley spoke of the rapidly growing ability of technology to identify potential hazards and the need to harmonize risk assessment and risk management approaches. He described the work of the Federal Coordinating Council for Science, Engineering, and Technology on risk assess-

Inconsistencies in risk management have undermined the credibility and effectiveness of risk regulation.

ment. The goal of this effort, coordinated by the Office of Science and Technology Policy, was described as the development of "a consensus on the assumptions and principles that should underlie the application of science and technology in support of risk management across the entire spectrum of the federal government."

Inconsistencies in both the scientific approaches and the policy approaches to risk management have undermined the credibility and effectiveness of risk regulation. Conflicting mandates have confounded the efforts of regulators and have been a source of frustration for the regulated community. The challenge for the future will be to achieve a more consistent scientific basis for decisions while recognizing the unique responsibilities and mandates of diverse agencies at the federal, state, and local levels.

DIRECTIONS FOR THE FUTURE

The participants in the "Regulating Risk" conference presented a rich variety of approaches to risk and recommendations for change. Despite the differences in approach and training, the most resounding theme of the conference was change. It appears that the time has come to reevaluate and refine the risk assessment and risk management approaches that have guided past risk management decisions. Regulating risk is by nature a dynamic process. To be successful the process not only must incorporate new scientific information but also must include consideration of developing public values and emerging economic realities.

Four specific themes for change that emerged from the conference have been presented in this chapter: strengthening the science, recognizing and incorporating public values, balancing costs, and harmonizing policies.

These themes can provide a template for revisiting the paradigm of the Red Book, which has guided the agencies for 10 years. It is time to refine the characterization of risks and to provide decision makers and the public with more complete information to guide the process.

The regulation of risk is an interaction of science, values, and economics. Ideally, science is the driving force behind regulation, with public values and economics providing guidance to decision makers. In the face of uncertainty in the science, however, it is all too possible for economics (costs?) and/or values (outrage?) to disrupt the balance of the decision-making process.

Achieving a better balance in risk regulation will require progress on many fronts. Risk regulation is a truly multidisciplinary problem requiring the integration of information from many sources. Historically, the process has been Balkanized by the viewpoints of the participating professional disciplines. The process requires the contribution of experts in many fields including scientists, economists, communication experts, lawyers, political experts, and public advocates. Unfortunately, there have been few opportunities for these disciplines to work together, and too often there has been an adversarial jockeying for position in the risk debate. At the conference, the tradition lived on—scientists criticized economists, communication experts criticized scientists, everyone criticized lawyers and politicians, and public advocates criticized everyone.

The conference reinforced the need to end the isolation of the disciplines, broaden the risk characterization process, and more clearly define the information needs of decision makers. Just as the Red Book provided a framework for risk assessment, there is a clear need to establish a similar framework or paradigm for risk management. The purpose of the paradigm would be to provide a more structured approach to balancing scientific and social considerations in risk decision making. The following "six-chair" approach represents an integration of the many recommendations offered at the conference and is offered as a starting point for discussion.

THE SIX-CHAIR APPROACH

Who would a decision maker want at the discussion table when faced with a difficult risk management decision?

Table 3. Six categories of risk management information

1. Science
   - Public health and ecological risks
   - Technical feasibility of risk management options

2. Law
   - Legislative mandates
   - Regulatory options

3. Economics
   - Costs and benefits
   - Economic feasibility of risk management options

4. Public Values
   - Public sensitivity to risk
   - Credibility of risk management options

5. Communication
   - Public involvement
   - Communication strategy for options

6. Politics
   - Political importance of risk
   - Political acceptability of options

Although public health protection may be the ultimate goal of the decision, an informed risk management decision requires sound information on all major factors that drive the regulatory process. Table 3 lists the categories of information recommended throughout the conference as necessary for an integrated approach to risk management. Under each category are two examples of the kind of information most useful in guiding the decision-making process. Additional categories may be appropriate, depending on the issue. This list is not intended to be all-inclusive.

Based on these categories, a roundtable discussion can be envisioned that could be called the "six-chair" approach to risk management. This suggests that the decision maker include six perspectives at the decision-making table. Paul Deisler, in his writings on the risk management–risk assessment interface, has similarly described the need for the risk manager to have a broad base of information. He points out that "all the needs of risk management are not satisfied merely by having available a sound scientific characterization of environmental health risks."[2] Such an approach would facilitate the discussion of the full realm of information essential to weave an effective approach to the regulation or management of risk. Figure 1 is an illustration of how a meeting between a policy decision maker and the "six chairs" might look.

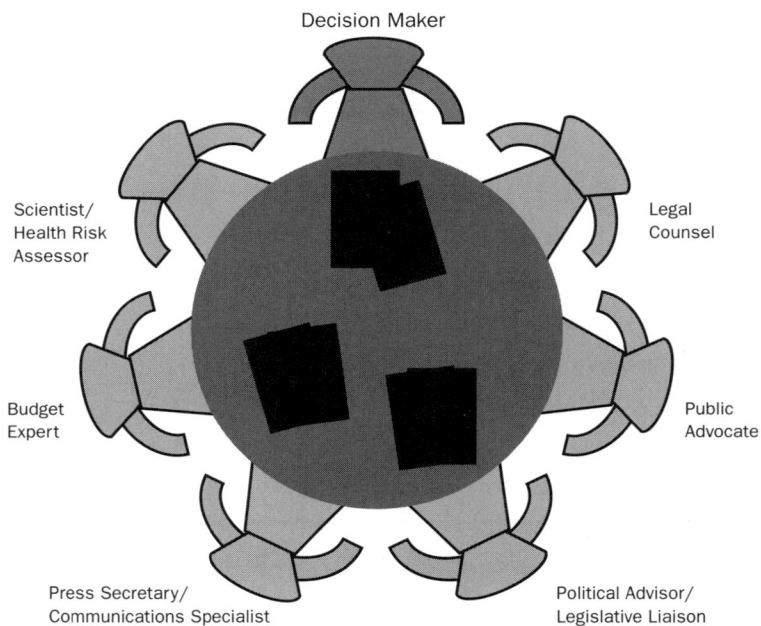

Figure 1. The "six chair" approach to risk management:
integrating the key perspective in the decision-making process

Although each of these "chairs" may currently play prominent roles in the risk decision-making process, there has been a lack of strategic integration. Thus, there are many examples of current risk regulation in which science, economics, or public values have not been appropriately integrated into the regulatory process. Recognition of types of information that shape risk decision making is an essential step toward developing a paradigm for risk management.

The regulation of risk is an interaction of science, values, and economics.

The success of future approaches to risk regulation may depend on recognition of the fundamental principles presented by Henry Habicht:

1. In a free society decision making resides in an informed public.
2. Safety or acceptable risk is not an objective scientific notion that is easily definable by experts.

Future approaches must better articulate the goals of risk management and meet the information needs of the decision makers and the public. This will require a multidisciplinary commitment to developing a refined framework for risk management. The themes for change that emerged from this conference represent the thoughts and recommendations of the leading authorities on risk science and risk policy from government, academia, and the business community. The themes provide a framework for achieving the ultimate goal of the "Regulating Risk" conference to advance the risk science and policy dialogue toward achieving a more balanced approach to regulating risk.

---

[1] Committee on the Institutional Means for Assessment of Risks to Public Health, National Research Council, National Academy of Sciences, *Risk Assessment in the Federal Government: Managing the Process* (Washington, DC: National Academy Press, 1983).

[2] Paul F. Deisler, Jr., "The Risk Management–Risk Assessment Interface," *Environmental Science and Technology* 22, no. 1 (January 1988): 15.

Thomas A. Burke, Ph.D., M.P.H., is an assistant professor in the Department of Health Policy and Management, Johns Hopkins University School of Hygiene and Public Health.

Regulating Risk:
The Science and Politics of Risk

Washington, D.C. ▪ June 24–25, 1991

ADVISORY COMMITTEE

FREDERICK W. ALLEN
Deputy Director, Science, Economics
    and Statistics Division
Office of Policy, Planning and Evaluation
Environmental Protection Agency

THOMAS A. BURKE, PH.D.
School of Hygiene and Public Health
Johns Hopkins University

BERNARD D. GOLDSTEIN, M.D.
Director, Environmental and
    Occupational Health Sciences
    Institute
UMDNJ–Robert Wood Johnson
    Medical School, Rutgers University

JOHN D. GRAHAM, PH.D.
Center for Risk Analysis
Harvard School of Public Health

PETER INFANTE, PH.D.
Director, Office of Standards Review
Occupational Safety and Health
    Administration

FRED A. MANUELE, CSP, P.E.
President, Hazards, Ltd.

ROBERT J. SCHEUPLEIN, PH.D.
Deputy Director, Toxicological Sciences
Center for Food Safety and Applied
    Nutrition
Food and Drug Administration

MICHAEL R. TAYLOR, ESQ.
King and Spalding

BUD WARD
Executive Director
Environmental Health Center
National Safety Council

Advisory Committee Cochairs:

JANE S. ROEMER, ESQ.
Executive Director, Public Policy
National Safety Council

CAROL J. HENRY, PH.D.
Executive Director
ILSI Risk Science Institute